Scarlet Cinders

a memoir

by

Martha Ann Letterman

Scarlet Cinders

a memoir by Martha Ann Letterman

First Edition

Published by Shelden Studios

PO Box 3221

Prince Frederick, Maryland 20678

ISBN 978-0-9977147-3-9

Printed in the United States of America

Opening

For all of my life I have had champions. These have been the people who have loved me, taught me, encouraged and supported me. This collection of memories is probably most effective when it is performed, but here, in this book, I am presenting it as a series of written vignettes about my early life.

I have collaborated with my sister Suzanne to publish it in this form, making it possible for me to finish the work and to share it in a style that a spoken word performance would not allow.

I want to thank my family and all the friends who have been there for me during this process. There are so many that in naming individuals, I risk forgetting someone. I will ask you to understand that without you this work would not have taken place. I know that you know who you are. Please know how grateful I am to you. This book is for you.

for my family

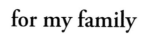

Why?

There comes a point in life, and I imagine it comes at a different time for each of us, when everything changes, and all that has come before seems to belong to a small box of memories, a time when it feels right to give thanks for the past and to let it go. This is such a moment for me. When I still wanted to be thought of, or remembered, for my efforts and the work of my early life, it was different. Now, I know that I cannot control the way I am viewed.

I suppose this might be my star turn. No longer "The Queen"—which is what my grandparents called me—I am reduced to a final five minutes of glamour in a theatre of memory alone. I can live with this. I can put on a lavender gown, pin a lilac sprig to my chest and sing out my soul. Then, I can put it all together in a suitcase, a box, a steamer trunk, and move it to a place of peace.

I have had a beautiful life. I have had the privilege to live fully, and to love deeply. Now, I have the chance to step to the side to encourage others in their walks down the earth.

Perhaps my walk is not finished. But now, as I take my heart to the hills, I find that there is no regret. If I hope for anything, it is that I will worry less. I would like to believe, finally, that I am enough. I realize there is no one way to live this last chapter, but the time has come to release the heavy weight of burdens collected along the way, so that, in the disarray of souvenirs cast at my feet, I can review the lessons learned and pass on my findings to those awaiting their turns, or to those already in the process of living their dreams.

Martha Ann Letterman

Contents

Spring Valley
Corey Place

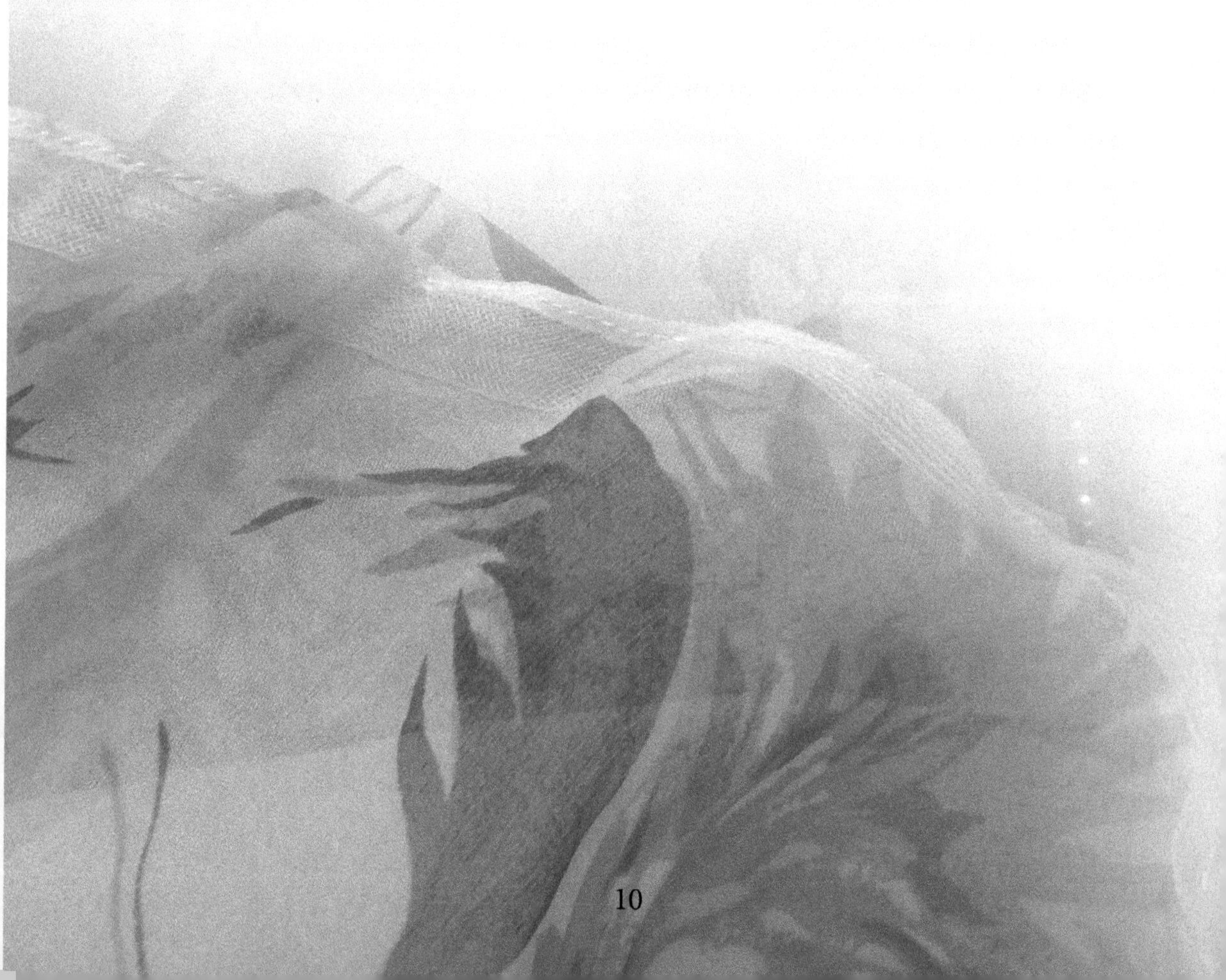

Spring Valley—Corey Place

Spring Valley — Corey Place

The Organdy Dress

I was a healthy baby in a white organdy dress with delicate lace trimmed sleeves, little satin roses in the front, and a big bow at the base of a row of six tiny mother of pearl buttons in the back.

I was a sweet, smiling, soft skinned little baby sitting content in a lovely, starched, dainty, visiting costume. I was a sturdy baby. But, I never thought, "What on earth is wrong with my chubby little fingers?"

I never said, "I should never have finished that Mapo. I don't care whose picture is at the bottom of that heated blue enamel bowl. I feel so fat in this dress."

No!

I just cooed and drooled a bit, feeling full of the comfort that came from being well loved, cared for, and fed.

The Birthday Parties

The table was set the night before with a special birthday party tablecloth. Placed on it would be plates, cups, hats and favors. My favorites of the latter were thin, plastic, powder pink and blue eyelet baskets with little swinging handles. These were for candy or special charms. I also liked the favors with the paper fringe on either end, which hid strips that popped like fire crackers when they were pulled.

Above the table, streamers and banners hung in tiers from the graduated crystal chandelier. The room looked like a tent. I felt like a nomad, a gypsy, and before I knew it, I secretly wanted to pack my bags and live in this way always.

The birthday cake was traditionally a Heidi Bakery birthday cake from the local Giant grocery store. I remember the cakes as yellow or white creations with butter cream frosting, a compound with which you could have plastered walls. The roses on the top were yellow, pink, red or white and had attached trailing vines and leaves of green.

The attire for these parties was formal. The girls wore fancy party dresses, each in their own style. We all had a signature, in those neighborhoods, by the time we were three years old. The boys wore wool pants or shorts with long knee socks and finishing touches of small sweaters or argyle vests over white shirts. Some of the boys had little jackets. The girls had jeweled sweaters, or plain ones with beaded angora collars, tiny fur wraps, or discrete miniature tailored jackets.

The gifts brought to these affairs by the little princes and princesses were fit for kings and queens. They were elaborately wrapped and expensive.

It was not a jolly, rollicking atmosphere. As I recall, it was one of quiet awe and open-eyed wonder at the beauty and splendor of these occasions. I do not think that I understood what I was seeing or experiencing. So young for all of this, I could very easily have become spoiled by it, but I was not. I believe I was just in a constant state of birthday surprise until I was about five years old, and the tides began to turn.

The Plaid Dresses and the Book Bag

Presto! These dresses arrived every year like clockwork. Clean, crisp, precise. Hunter green, navy blue, and red, they were white collared plaid creations for elementary school days. These dresses were so stiff they practically stood at attention. In companionship with double-buckled book bags, notebooks, special roll-topped pencil cases, and the occasional pen—I was marching to a tune of success.

These were ensembles of promise and new beginnings for scholarship in the early days of life. Together with my classmates, I depended upon the strong personality of my outfits and made my entrances to school as if to the accompaniment of bagpipes, a small Scott in a Military Tattoo.

The Set

I lived in an urban forest within the city, a setting that was predisposed to be magical. My house was a solid, well-built home typical of the 1940s.

Beautifully decorated in a simple but elegant style, the lower floors were papered with silk-flocked wall paper, with a raised layer of material which felt like velvet. There were unusual and creative wall papers in the first floor bathroom and in the children's rooms upstairs. On the second floor these papers featured exotic birds, circus animals and bubbles.

Heavy doors led to the outdoor and porch areas from the front hall, living room and kitchen. Inside, were lovely multi-paned windows with venetian blinds, chandeliers, homey 1950s appliances and decor in the kitchen, richly-colored oriental carpets covering the floors, and a Ma Bell telephone that answered to the number of Emerson 2-4795.

Gold-plated floral wedding plates were on display in the breakfront. On the buffet, an impressive silver service found a home. The dining room furniture, in the Duncan Phyfe style, had a drop leaf table and a graceful set of matching chairs upholstered in a striped fabric of green and champagne satin. Wine-red velvet drapes hung in the dining and living rooms and met the floors of gleaming oak with an extra foot of fan-shaped material.

In every corner of every room and surface there seemed to be scent. It could be floor wax, perfume, talcum powder, lemon oil, simmering stew, coffee, hot chocolate or aftershave, evergreen or holiday pine. It could be shampoo suds, laundry detergent, sizzling steak, baking bread, warming meatloaf with tomato sauce, paste from a school project, vinegar and Easter egg dye, eggnog with sprinkles of nutmeg, hot tea with tart lemon squeezed into it, sugar cookies, gingerbread or mother's barbecued spare ribs. It could be the diaper pail, lipstick, hairspray, falling snowflakes, a Thanksgiving Day turkey, a Christmas ham, turpentine, Old Spice Cologne or Shalimar Eau De Cologne. It could be cigarette and cigar smoke or lavender sachet. It could be all of these. What it was—was home.

Christmas

Christmastime on Corey Place in Northwest Washington, DC set the bar for all holiday seasons to come. Until my mother died in 2008, I still felt the familial tone she set for us all those years ago. My early time between 1948 and 1958 held the most magic. Our house, from my earliest memory, was one of great love and giving. It was also one of an abiding and overpowering anguish. One aspect could not cancel out the other. Each coexisted, holding home between them. At Christmastime there was a loosening of this bondage, and I, mercifully, could breathe.

My parents were wonderful people who tried and did their best to care and to provide for us. We were offered rare, often unusual, opportunities. But, my parents were in over their young heads and were coping with an onslaught of addictions compounded by the demands of the lifestyle in which they found themselves. At Christmastime they too had a reprieve, seeming to come alive with the relief and spiritual abundance of the time of year.

We had advent calendars shining with snowy glass glitter, Sundays in church school with services held in the glorious, gothic, architectural masterpiece: The United Methodist Metropolitan Memorial Church, on Nebraska Avenue in Northwest Washington, DC. We had snowmen and angels in the yard, and blue, green, orange, yellow, red, and white grooved teardrop Christmas lights on the entrance railing to our house.

A wreath of evergreen hung on the front door, decorated with a great big red all-weather bow. Inside the house, fragrances of warm food and sounds of traditional holiday music filled the air. We had rituals of reading and story telling. With the arrival of television, we enjoyed holiday movies, cartoons and Christmas specials. Mostly, there was the belief and the accompanying hope that all would be well.

It could have been the setting, or maybe it was just that first morning of full discovery that opened the portals of Christmas for me. The light came from candles and from the branches of the Christmas tree, with its colorful bulbs and bubbling lights. The look of Christmastime in our house was a tantalizing declaration of magic. The details so haltingly lovely that looking around at them was like a dream from which I never wanted to awaken.

The memory of crawling onto the rug or walking on newly tested limbs with this over me was like entering a magic woodland. Tinsel touched my head like long silver raindrops. The aroma of evergreen boughs draped me in a haze of enchantment. I was a captive of its unique festivity.

The Christmas tree was the centerpiece of the season. Finding it, bringing it home, and choosing a place for it were all events that were part of a calming ritual. Whether pine, fir, or spruce—the evergreen fragrance was a hallmark of the season ahead. Ornaments of the Shiny Brite vintage would suddenly appear from their places of storage with "friends," other vintage Christmas balls and bells of all varieties. Garland and tinsel were the favored finishing touches and oddly, they were usually quibbled over, especially the tinsel. The lighting was provided by colorful liquid bubble lights shaped like tops and the ridged lights in strands that were miniature versions of the outside variety: tiny teardrops of white, green, red, gold and blue.

In the living room were my grandparents, Georgie and Jack, my parents, Doris and John, and Gail and Johnny, my little sister and my younger brother. From floor to ceiling, from under the tree and spreading to every corner of the room were a multitude of lavishly wrapped presents.

All kinds of papers had been used in the six month preparation for this display: tissue, printed papers with snow scenes, churches with lighted steeples, Santa and his tiny reindeer, pastoral villages, holiday decorations, cookies and candy canes. There were plain and striped heavy foil wrappings in shiny red, emerald green, royal blue, silver, gold, and peacock. Some of the lighter foils were etched with delicate patterns. The bows on the packages were fashioned with fabrics of all sizes, weights and thicknesses. Their shared aspect was that they were elegant and artistically made.

Hardly ever, for me, was this about the unimaginable bounty beneath the tree in those boxes and bags or hanging from the mantle in the stockings. It was about the beauty. The magic created in our house was full of such a desperate hope it all but shimmered.

I have seen and participated in many Christmas celebrations, but there has never been anything like crossing the Corey Place living room threshold on my first remembered Christmas morning. If this memory were an old-time movie, it would be a magenta 16 mm film strip of wonder.

My Mother's Closet

My mother's closet was an intimate theatre whose highly polished floor welcomed me with its accommodating spaciousness. On one side was evening wear, on the other, everyday clothes. In the winter the everyday side allowed space for coats. The evening clothes needed their own domain in all seasons. Shoes were set in order on racks beneath the clothing on both the left and the right. Hats were in boxes of many shapes in a two-doored cabinet above the closet. On each side of the closet above the garments were built in shelves. Here, pocketbooks and evening bags were placed.

In my mother's room, there was always fragrance. Expensive, sometimes French, it was always beautiful. These were potent scents. Neither light, flowery or green, nor as heavy as incense, they were dramatic and exotic without being too overpowering. Shalimar, Golliwog, Chanel N°5, and Miss Dior were among her favorites.

So it was that amid the beeswax and perfume, I nestled into a veritable treasure trove of costumes. Wools, gabardines, taffetas, shantungs, voiles, old wood fiber rayons, silks, velvets, tulles, crepes, chiffons and fur were used to fashion the clothing and the coats. Each garment promised a moment of style to come, which, once rendered in the world, could never be repeated.

The handbags were made of bakelite, plastic, suede, calf leather, fabric, patent leather, tapestry, crepe, metal, silk, beads, mesh, lizard, crocodile, python, and alligator. Who needed the Everglades? We had our own reptiles. Our swamp—the closet!

There were plastic slippers encrusted with rhinestones heightened with sculptured lucite heels. These shoes previewed the gorgeous parade of spiked heels to come—an array so colorful and varied in design, texture, and ornament, you could have dined on their allure alone.

Most fondly, I recall the ballerina length, cotton, summer, dinner-dance dresses. They were fitted off the shoulder confections in every color and imaginable print with multi-tiered full-skirted petticoats. They were designed with a graceful, trim-figured woman in mind, tailored to suit an individual with plans and social engagements. I lived in waiting for these occasions and the preparations they often involved, hoping, in my heart, for them to go on . . . endlessly.

The Martini Stain

It was there, just like that. One day an expanse of beige carpet, the next day an expanse of beige carpet with an irregular shaped, vivid orange stain. At various times, I attacked it. My allies in these exertions were Oxydol, Clorox, Bon Ami, Borax and even Fels-Naptha soap. Even Ivory Soap flakes were enlisted to assist me as I tried to remove the spot from the rug.

This was a copper orange blight on the living room floor. It did not match the wine-red drapes, the soft ivory brocade wing chairs, or the burgundy velour couch with the corded fringe. The stain was visible from the hallway entrance to the living room. It was about eight feet from the edge and could not be missed from any angle when entering or exiting the room. Facing it, or passing it by, the disturbance was the same. The truth of the matter being, there was worry ahead.

I could say that I was too young to know when it started, the trouble. But, young or old, in our house, we knew. It was our secret. No one spoke of it, but we all felt it inside, and once the stain appeared in our midst, our worlds turned.

At some point another layer was laid over the beige carpet. The rug was an exquisite deep piled Oriental with intricate designs in shades and hues of blue, brown, violet, and orange. No matter how rich, luxurious, or thick this covering was, in that one spot—eight feet in—the color seemed brighter. It was almost a vibration. This was no ordinary stain. This was an alert, a warning of danger ahead. I just sat in silence and waited for it to come.

Little Zenith

In the '50s in America many homes had television sets. By 1953, I had one, too, waiting for me under the Christmas tree in the living room. There it was. This big package, wrapped in silver paper, was trimmed with a broad red ribbon tied in a fancy bow. I opened the box with help from my parents. All eyes were upon me. What could this be, I wondered?

Well . . .

Out from the trappings came a miniature television set. This was the biggest thing ever to me, at five years old.

The set, which bore the label Zenith, was black, and about nineteen inches long. It had a muted gold metal border, framing a small smoky-green screen. The set tilted up and down, making it tailor-made for me to watch my favorite shows while it sat on my bedside table. It looked like a sports car.

This beautiful little appliance was my first really big surprise, a gift from Santa Claus who I believed in, and still do, all of these years later.

By two nights after this Christmas morning, the television had settled into its new home in my childhood room with its pink and blue bubble wallpaper. On this particular evening, there was a holiday party for my parents to attend. I always loved watching them getting ready to go out. My father would be wearing an evening suit, or a tuxedo. My mother would be in a cocktail dress, or a formal gown. The atmosphere was layered with the spirit of preparation, cologne and perfume. I was happy too, because I had my little TV.

Before my parents left for the evening, I was given orders to turn the set off at 9:30 ON THE DOT. I lost track of time as I was immersed in the joy of watching the seasonal specials. All of a sudden, I heard raised voices. Now that I knew my parents were home, I quickly turned off the television set with the button on the control panel. In those times you had to wait for two things to happen. One was for the picture tube to fade from a bright to a dim orange, then to a flickering, faint, soft apricot. Two was for the set to cool down. My little set was still a hot fading orange. I had not been quick enough.

My father appeared in the door of my room with my mother behind him, frantically speaking in a raised voice. He was very angry with me, saying that I was disobedient and ungrateful. Furiously, he took my little set from its perch and, with the full force of his weight, threw it down the main staircase of our house on Corey Place in Spring Valley in Northwest Washington, DC, two evenings after Christmas morning.

Its parts scattered like the beads of a broken necklace to the far corners of the first floor. Some, which rolled free, landed homeless under the, still lit, fragrant tree and were reflected in the bright metallic colorful balls that hung from the low branches.

The little Zenith never worked well after that.

I felt so sorry for the little Zenith, for I knew this was my fault. As the fragments of my Christmas present cascaded to the edges of the house, upstairs my mother was repeatedly beaten to the floor. When the last part rolled still and my mother's cries subsided, I squeezed my eyes together and slept. Guilty as charged. This was the last night of my childhood.

A Stitch in Time

Some days, I just didn't know what to do first. My job at home was beyond my years and I had no experience to meet its challenges. As is so often the case, the solutions do come if you are in tune with your surroundings. Even so young, I was strung like a harp. Every plucked string sounded an instruction. This one came in a small Christmas box, a surprise package. Inside was a new set of garments for understanding and arranging time.

Were I to have any doubt of my direction, I could stand in the path of any mirror and twirl around. I could then read information that would tell me which chores I needed to perform, if it was time to play, go to school, appear in church, or visit a friend.

What a whirlwind! With this special set of reminders, I had a direction. At seven, and in a set of seven, they came to me one for each day of the week. On each pastel set of "drawers" was stitched in color: Sunday, Monday, Tuesday, Wednesday, Thursday, Friday, Saturday—written on pink, yellow, white, pale blue, mint green, ivory and lavender nylon.

These stitches were under my skirt, but they were a map of the order of my world.

Radio Drama

My one perfect moment with the world of old time radio came when I had the measles as a child. Each of the children in our house had a case, one right after the other, and we all had the same sick room. The room, at the time, was my brother John's room. There were wonderful yellow draperies with jungle and circus animals: giraffes, lions, zebras, tigers and bears. In the corner was a Walt Disney log cabin cardboard playhouse. I was not one for playing in the house, plagued with the measles as I was, but I loved the safari atmosphere created by the darkened room and the fabric animals. It was in this nocturnal scene that I was tucked in, served meals and checked upon. One week I saw my mother's notes on a chart that tracked "the children's illnesses" . . . and noted that I had experienced a "light case" and was deemed to be "a very good patient."

The chief memory of my reward for good behavior was the Philco radio by my bedside. This one had a little red bar that indicated the channel on which I would soon be hearing: Dragnet, Amos 'n' Andy, Young Dr. Malone, The Romance of Helen Trent, and other period shows.

There were whole worlds of voice theatre right at my bedside. In the soft filters of the, no light, measles bedchamber, these characters cast a brightness on my convalescence. Even at that early age they created a love and a deep understanding of the message that could be carried by the spoken word. My inspiration came then as a gift, transmitted over the airwaves, begetting my desire to create by speaking in Radio Drama.

The Blue Dress with The Banner and the Three Big White Buttons

"Too much foolishness," it read, in red, across the pages of my report card. This was delivered in a five-by-seven envelope by my third-grade teacher, Mrs. McGee.

By the time I was in the third grade, I had begun my eleven-year tour of duty as the clown. I was the funny one, joking around in order to be accepted. A lot of this "fun" took place in a balloon shaped dress of an aquamarine color. There was a three-inch banner across the front. This was exactly the same size that was fitted for our Girl Scouts uniform. I knew that it read "Big Fat Pig." They had already started calling me names. I just didn't know what to do. Food had become my companion, my comfort, and my best friend. I just kept getting fatter and funnier by the day. Although my weight went up and down until my college graduation, I consistently played my part as the clown.

And then . . . a friend rescued me. She was angry with me at the time for a turn of adult foolishness made at her expense the prior evening. She simply looked at me in my dark brown, low cut velveteen cocktail dress, and said coolly, and in disgust, "You are like a big blow up clown endlessly taking punches to the ground from others and from yourself. One of these days, you are going to go down and never come back up again."

That was it.

My career as the fool was over. I was thin, but at that moment, I felt like the overweight child in the blue dress with the banner and the three big white buttons. I knew that I had been given a second chance for self esteem.

Cleaning the Porch

When the thick, many-paned, glass door cracked open with that bright peeling sound like leaves brittle with fall, to reveal the blue-grey, ridged, painted floor of my screened in porch, and I saw, out of the corner of my eye, the appearance of tiny green buds with perfect yellow flowers on the forsythia bushes that ranged in clusters along my sloping driveway, I knew it would soon be time.

I had long been waiting for this moment to arrive and I was ready for our ritual of preparing the three-sided, double-paned, screened-in porch for the changing season. Out came the buckets, and the soap, and the mops, and the bristles. I became a pastel witch, eager to ride my broom across this road to spring. I flew in big sweeping patterns across the floor to wash the cement surfaces, which were now foaming like high tide.

Next came the drying of the walls and the gleaming floors. The glinting water in the tiny mesh of the screens would form patterns. I was an artist, that was it, and now standing on my damp grey pond, I could view my wire masterpieces until twilight.

Through the curtained porch door, lights softened by pleated white gauzy sheers cast incandescent filters on this industry. Now, I was a lightning bug, darting about, glimmering with expectation.

So it was that I would "play house." inspired by the interior decoration of my home, I would plan new arrangements for our glass, wrought iron, wicker, metal, and bamboo porch furniture.

As I worked, I would mentally preview outdoor pleasures: cool iced drinks, bookmobile book reading, paper dolls, board games, trading cards, hobbies, and summer weight blankets. The enchantment of my seasonal house was a cinematic tableau of spring and summer living in an urban forest.

This was our Spring Valley, with its iris, honeysuckle, lilacs and daffodils, the sounds of birds chirping and singing in the trees, the busily buzzing bees, and the crisp deafening whir of cicadas in the bushes. This was the lazy, sultry, soothing, almost embalming sound of my childhood hours.

The Trading Cards

Trading cards were among my prized possessions. I kept them in boxes: cigar boxes, shoe boxes or gift boxes, depending upon the size of the collection. I collected, sorted, and traded images of horses, cats, dogs, flowers, floral designs, birds, pinups, ballerinas, cowboys and indians, houses, and country scenes. I shared these activities with my neighborhood friends on porches, in kitchens, on living room floors, in backyards, and in the woods.

I found the cards at our local hobby store, Homewood Hardware, and at a smaller shop across from the National Zoo in Woodley Park. They were playing card size and had no writing on the back. Some earlier vintage cards had advertisements, but these were not among the ones familiar to me.

I guarded my collection and carried it around with me in a box, changing the order and position of the cards so often that their edges became as smooth as velvet.

These images, so collectible at the time, are difficult to track down in any quantity today. It sometimes feels as though they have disappeared, or that I only imagined their existence.

Paper Dolls

To put a spotlight on it, playing with paper dolls was one of the pastimes I enjoyed the most. Some dolls could be punched out of a slightly perforated paper. Others I would need to cut out, following bold or dotted lines. Although the punched out variety were easier to assemble for play, the ones I cut out proved to be the most rewarding. Here, as I carefully cut the outfits and arranged them into categories, I found that I could plan entire wardrobes and scenarios for my beloved paper pals.

I can still remember the imprint the sisal rugs made on my legs, as I sat for hours on our screened porch with these books and scissors and boxes of paper clothing, crafting lifestyles for the dolls. Like the trading cards I collected and played with during the same period, these paper dolls were items for the porches and back steps. These quiet, imaginative activities later added to my character. As I grew up, I became that paper doll, trying on those paper outfits as occasions changed, and as, step by step, I took center stage.

Now I Lay Me Down to Sleep

Every night, we children got down on our knees to pray. Our little prayer: "Now I lay me down to sleep. I pray the Lord my soul to keep. If I should die before I wake, I pray the Lord my soul to take."

This was the ritual throughout our childhood. Were we religious? Not per se. We went to church and to Sunday school regularly, but these evening prayers were a thing apart. Considering this now, I think this was our mother's beloved faith reaching out to us through the storm of our early lives. Not all dark, our lives were a mixture, chiaroscuro. This prayer came each evening, bringing peace to my heart. No matter what the day had held, this was my gateway to night.

I have a little book left behind by my mother. It is filled with quotes from the Bible, anonymous sayings, and bits of poetry. Some of these were in print, cut out of a newspaper or magazine, and some, in her time of meditation and deep thought, she copied over word for spiritual word. I believe my mother was religious. She guided our activities in this quarter but really did not, at least to me, give voice to her own beliefs. I do not know if I would have heard it anyway. I was selfish and self-centered, or maybe I was just afraid. I suppose that it was the way I had to be at the time. I am sorry for this now. I wish I had known my mother better than our circumstances allowed.

In the later years, I did share the truth, the quiet, and love with her. That is a blessing. I feel rich to have this book of her private writings. I wonder now, as I lay my weary head down each evening, if one day someone will find my writings and wonder about me, too. I do know that there is no forcing this, the wanting of care from others. The world is a complex and busy place and I am grateful there are a few who reach out to me and wish to know. If I should die before I wake, I know that they know who they are and will realize how life-saving their concern and loving attentions were.

In life, as I now understand it, the beauty of this intimacy, this offering of undefended friendship, is ministry. It seems to be a way, in these unusual times, to value others, and to acknowledge, with each passing moment, the power of a shared history.

All of this harkens back to my own dear mother, who, hearing the silent, early cries of our confusion, offered a solution she understood deeply: prayer.

The White Elephant Sale

Help was on the way. I knew it the moment I arrived to work at the tables of our third grade White Elephant Sale. There they were, items lined up on the tables, in various shapes, designs and colors. I looked at these treasures and felt, suddenly: comfort, safety, humor, charm, and something almost sacred.

I sensed that these displaced articles understood me. We were comrades, foot soldiers, record keepers. They, too, were veterans of the domestic war and peace of the 1950s, witnesses to the dramatic beauty and torment of our first neighborhoods and their residential interiors. We shared these experiences, silently trading our stories, all variations of the same one.

A bond was formed. Each item I sold or kept was the same, a piece of my heart, staying or going. We were now rendered transients, positioned only as visitors. The longing borne of this new recognition was like a herald signaling a hope, trumpeting a song of home. A love grew between us. Each forgotten tea cup, discarded dresser box, set of glasses or dishes, empty perfume bottle, abandoned toy, hand mirror, bowl, doily, or china figurine was a partner in my trek out of a jungle of confusion, disorientation, and grief. Each white elephant, my white knight.

Situation Comedy

Amos 'n' Andy, Love that Bob, The Eve Arden Show, My Little Margie, I Love Lucy, Our Miss Brooks, The Ann Southern Show, December Bride, Oh Susanna! Television! I loved snow or sick days in the '50s and early '60s. I would begin my living room viewing with the morning talk and news shows, which I endured as a sort of penance. What followed were the game shows and then the line-up of situation comedies. As these commenced, the fun would carry me right up to *The Early Show* in the evening.

The characters in these shows became my friends and neighbors, much like the dynasties of families I read about in historical romance novels today. As a solitary individual, even then, these people offered me community, an extended family of sorts. They delivered ideas about homemaking, social circumstance, friendship, clothing, and domestic behavior. As I grew up, of course, the shows changed. Now we had *The Mary Tyler Moore Show, The Bob Newhart Show, The Partridge Family, My Three Sons*, and *The Beverly Hillbillies*. But it was those early morning and afternoon shows that snapped the lasting pictures for my wallet.

Queen For a Day

Why on earth would I not have grown up with a taste for drama? One of the many shows I watched as a child was *Queen for a Day.* I believe this show was one of those that would later be called a "Misery Show." On the aired segment, a series of contestants would each tell their story, which was usually quite the tale of woe! The audience would then vote as to whose situation was the worst, via an applause meter. The saddest story won the prize.

In my life, I did not need to travel far for a story of this kind. But I wonder if somehow that early measure of sadness on the television set me up to glorify the experience of being a victim, rendering me an individual waiting for rescue, living as a martyr without reprieve.

For the show, I believe these stories were devised as a performance style and a structure geared to the advertising of products.

For me, it was something different. At the very least, I could watch this contest, perhaps seeing that I was not the only one, and that, someday, if I were to find a way to describe what I felt, there might be others who would understand. Then, I, too, could be Queen for a Day.

The Berkshire and the Greenbriar

They were side by side, with just enough space between them so that they each held their own dignity. These were two apartment buildings on the left side of the street, south of Ward Circle, in the District of Columbia of my youth.

They exist today, positioned as student housing and apartments for young professionals. Even all of those years ago, these two structures seemed poised for a long run. They stood solid and still, amidst the shrubbery, planted trees and flower beds that were part of their richly textured urban landscaping. Both had grand, sweeping circular driveways.

The Berkshire was the farthest south and the more masculine of the two. By their locations alone, they had an air of elegance and prestige. When we approached to pick up a friend of my parents, it was as if we had been suddenly cast in an old time movie and now had Cole Porter piano music coursing through our veins. This was especially true when driving up to the Greenbriar. When evening came, the light changed to a soft lavender glow with amber and golden highlights.

The female inhabitants of these dwellings would emerge in tweeds, taffetas and in tulles of emerald green, brown, pale yellow, and deep burgundy and carried with them an air of romance. We could hear the clicking of their old fashioned high heels as they passed us. In their speaking gait, these people forecasted that they were headed for something, or someone, with promise. It was the same with the men in their suits, top coats, hats and wing tip shoes. They had flair with a smoldering twist and not a care in the world, it seemed.

I can only sigh and celebrate that very brief window of luxury, beauty and emotional privilege we enjoyed as we approached the Berkshire and the Greenbriar.

The Cocktail Parties

We lived on a cul-de-sac. In our neighborhood, Spring Valley, in the summertime, it was customary for most of the families who lived on the circle, and some whose backyards bordered these homes, to host early evening cocktail parties.

The adults, now finally home for the day, would get ready to go out. There would be an early dinner and then a baby sitter would come to the house. There were shows to watch, games to play, and the familiar anticipation of seeing my parents as they put on their best clothes. Their good-byes would come with clouds of perfume and aftershave.

The moment I loved best on these occasions came when they left for the party. I would choose the window in the house that was positioned closest to where the engagement was taking place. I would sit by the window in a chair, or, if the party was next door, quietly in the shadows on the screened-in porch to listen to the sounds of the unfolding evening. It always began quietly with cricket song. It was almost as if you could hear the humid air, a voice or two, or a sigh raised above nature's song. Then, moments of silence and peace with an occasional snippet of conversation, or the distant tinkling of glassware with ice, or the popping corks of bottles of champagne, so still was the night.

Then, all of a sudden, the chatter would become clearer, offering a consistent palette of mirth, gaiety and the occasional bark of sophisticated laughter. It was relaxing and comfortable to sit like this and imagine the fun my parents must be having. It almost felt like I was there myself.

I believe now it was the same story each time. I would be mesmerized by the cadence of the sounds and would drift off for a little nap. Then, it always happened this way, I would be jolted awake.

The sounds were louder now and the glass heard seemed, not to be the sound of a glass tinkling with ice and spirits, but of sheets of broken glass and many raised voices, usually male. The females made their own contributions in a high soprano. It was as if sirens screamed through the hot air. And then I would hear it—The Sound. It would come from below, or beside me, if I was downstairs on the porch. This must be the reason that whenever I hear an emergency vehicle, I think they are coming to my house; to put out the fire, or to take me away.

In the case of these evenings, it would be my parents coming home, escorted by an assortment of gentlemen from their circle of friends, making certain that they made it into the house. Then the door shutting, then, SILENCE. Then, it would begin. The fighting and screaming and weeping and the broken dishes. My lullaby of domestic violence.

I was hidden, by now, still as a stone, scared, scarred, to death. The wonder of the quiet warm evening delight of the cocktail symphony long, long gone.

Brigadoon

It is not an uncommon story that a world of relief could be found by life as it was depicted in the early film musicals. As a child from a troubled home, this was certainly true for me. I realized this, when going to the movies began to save my life. The movie musicals did the trick. *Carousel, Oklahoma, The King and I, Silk Stockings, Damn Yankees, Brigadoon, Pal Joey,* and *The Pajama Game* were among my favorites.

The neighborhood theatre was an art deco jewel called The Apex Theatre. It was elegant. The upstairs lounges were decorated in shades of pink and mossy green. They had pretty carpeting and period light fixtures. There was even a crying room. Popcorn was dispensed from a machine for 25 cents and came in a red and white paper bag. I would crawl into my seat as if it was a lifeboat, and that may have been exactly it was. I learned all the songs and fantasized that I had the voice, the clothes, and the lives of these people. This was magic. It was colorful, dramatic and full of hope. The charm of the settings and landscapes on the screen were irresistible. I believe that I was drawn most dramatically and romantically to *Carousel*. It was light and dark at the same time. This struck home. I understood it. But it was the mystical *Brigadoon* that stole my soul. Here was the promise of a place apart where miracles could occur, somewhere between what was real and what was fantasy. I wanted it. This was similar to the feeling I had when Peter Pan flew. I knew that, if I were a good enough girl, I would be able to fly too. I would go into my bedroom, close the door, climb up on the bed and leap into the air. Now, I believed that when I crossed the bridge to *Brigadoon*, I would be able to dance, to love, to sing and to disappear.

These early movies gave a face to my dreams and an industry to follow. They gave me an appreciation of form and beauty, a love for the allure of glamour and romance (that might not have been such a great idea), an immediate identification with a variety of feelings, and a new brush to paint with. The movies were strokes of genius, creating worlds that I needed. They changed me for the better and went on to inspire and save me every day of my life.

Cotillion

I thought it was for learning to dance: Cotillion. Thinking back, I believe it was an introduction to formal society, to manners, and to aspects of decorum.

Recently, I passed by the place where the Cotillions were held. I saw the Wesley Heights Community Center, the little brick building on the corner behind the Horace Mann School. It is now boarded up on the lower side around the corner from its entrance, and I could see, on the floor above, fluorescent lights where the old rustic chandeliers used to hang.

As I closed my eyes, it could have been yesterday that I rounded this corner to go to ballet school, and later to Cotillion, to dance foxtrots, waltzes and cha cha chas. Where I now stood had been the Wesley Heights Drug Store next to a small neighborhood grocery store. I remembered all of the times at the old soda fountain, ordering a cherry smash, and the fun it was to buy magazines and candy.

Remembering Cotillion: It had coat rooms, receiving lines, hand shakes, party dresses, white gloves, ballroom chairs, rustic chandeliers, creaking wooden floors, young boys and girls, curtsies and bows, conversations, giggles and perfume, tears, friendships, and light betrayals. Rising and falling from the dance, within all of this, I made the passage from my childhood to my preteen years.

The details of living that I learned seemed to fill in my awkward blanks with a set of new rules and guidelines. I was thus led onto a path, an avenue to the particulars of a world that required the pause and poise of refinement. Not all of our numbers accepted the way shown. Some did, while others crept along the sidelines, looking in, as if from a dense wood, feeling unworthy of the chances that were being offered, preferring instead, the half truths and the excesses of life lived in the shadows.

Two Dresses

There were these two boxes. They were from Julius Garfinckel and Company. Two deep, white boxes with lids in midnight blue with gold lettering. This was 1957. I was nine years old. For my birthday party, all of my guests and I were taken to see Walt Disney's *Fantasia* at the Warner movie theatre downtown near the White House. These two boxes loomed large in my mind throughout the feature presentation.

When I got home and my friends departed, I went upstairs to my room to look more carefully at my birthday presents. They were beautifully wrapped gifts from my favorite department store. Inside of the boxes were two dresses. One was a baby blue polished cotton dress with a scooped neckline and one inch shoulder straps. There was a zipper down the back, and a belt, which was covered in fabric like my mother's belts. Fastened at the side with a silver plated pin was a delicate pink nosegay. The second belted dress was beige, but a beautiful peach-toned beige with a dark brown rick rack for trim. This dress was a duplicate of the pattern of the first. Although it was the plainer of the two, the dress somehow held its own. This was probably because of the rick rack.

These were beautiful creations, fresh and spring-like. This however, was November. There was stormy weather outside, but the message that accompanied these two boxes was as clear as a summer's day.

I stood in my black and white, big-squared, taffeta-plaid, full-skirted party dress with its petticoats and bodice of black velveteen. In this, I felt, and most certainly looked, chubby, gazing in wonderment and trepidation at the message emanating from the birthday boxes. "IF . . . you are very good, these two dresses that cost a fortune might fit you by springtime. You really must watch your weight, Martha Ann."

The Chinese Chimes

I have tried to recapture them in my mind for years. I used to buy them from G.C. Murphy and Company and Kresge's. Today one must go very far, to the outer reaches of nowhere, to find and recreate this shopping experience. I admit, many years later, that I am still this little girl dressed in beautiful clothing, wandering up and down the aisles of the old five and dime store searching for treasure. I recall from these wooden aisles: diaries, autograph books, stationery, makeup bags, Evening in Paris cologne, perfumes by Coty, lipsticks galore, jewelry, marbles, pencil cases, turtles and fish, finger toys, TinkerToys, fans, linens, underwear, pajamas, paper lanterns, birthday decor, paper cups and plates and a myriad of other delights.

The chinese chimes came in a box and cost about 75 cents. Something about them spoke to me. I never wanted to be without at least one box in reserve. Today they are called "Vintage Chinese Glass Wind Chimes." They were miniature glass plates, held together by tiny red silk strings. The panes of glass were about three inches long and were hand painted with little dashes of color in pale shades of yellow, red, aqua, green, and white. The delicate faint stokes of color contrasted with the thin, bright red strings.

Having gone online in a modern shopping search, I was delighted to find a community of devotees chatting about these creations, and was comforted that objects of my fond memories were valued by others.

In this moment I shed some of the self-consciousness I felt over the whimsical things I cherish, and began to write about the magical pieces of my life, acknowledging 'my personal opera,' whose composition seemed underscored by a higher being. The unholy sounds of shattering glass and china from my home were met with another sound, one of a light tinkling grace, one almost delivered to help me give thanks for what might one day come from navigating the rivers of emotional extremes. This glass music instilled in me the faith to reach for the waiting miracle of life as it might be led.

Valentines Day

Will you be mine? Be my Valentine. Bundles of red and white cards seasonally carried messages to families and secret loves. Under the heady umbrella of deep winter stillness came these lacy paper tapestries. This is where it all began. The deep attachment to longing and to the pain of loneliness. The possibility of being saved was compelling, attractive, and powerful. This is what I craved as a child, a teenager and especially as an emerging adult. It became my most important and closely guarded secret. Love was going to save me. Wanting it and waiting for it was the answer.

Dressed to the nines in RED, I sat poised, as a child, while carefully writing each word, and as a teen, crafting more closely knit phrases designed to lasso romance. These efforts later paved the way for much longer poems. These were really landscapes of desire written to attract the missing pieces of my puzzle.

And so every year I cut my heart out of paper and cast my fate to the wings of these posted messages—and then I stood still hoping I might at last be called someone's sweetheart.

This rarely happened and I was, over time, left with the memory of words sent and piles of paper that were the hallmarks of my attempts to arrange intimate conversations and commitments and love.

Valentine's Day can be a wonderful occasion to remember others in your heart. All by itself it can simply be a day to say to anyone you choose: you are special to me, I cherish you, and I hear you, and I would like you to be my Valentine.

The Easter Baskets

Every Easter morning, before we went off to church, we would arise early to go downstairs and look for our Easter baskets. These delightful surprises were left during the night by the Easter Bunny, or so we were told.

By now the sun was beaming through the venetian blinds lighting a path to our surprises. In our early years, this was the custom. In those days we were three on the hunt and would find these gifts behind the couch, behind the living or dining room drapes, or sometimes for fun, almost in plain sight on a tabletop in the living room. These baskets were—there is no other way to put it—exquisite.

They were wrapped in triple weight cellophane with beautiful purple bows, and inside them we found chocolate bunnies, bright yellow foam chicks, expensive jelly beans, individually wrapped chocolate eggs covered in delicate mint green, raspberry, gold, silver, and ice blue foils. There was usually a beautiful egg fashioned of glittering sugar, detailed with a hardened frosting, framing a clear window through which you could see Easter and spring dreamscapes.

Sometimes in addition to these extravagant displays there would be a real bunny rabbit, or a triplet of baby chicks, come to live with us.

Over the years these traditions continued. But as time went on, the detail and lavish optimistic style of their beginnings faded.

The Attic

This was a library of sorts, cataloging the past and the future simultaneously. A place where clothing, shoes, luggage, old furniture, Christmas decor, Easter baskets, furs, gowns, coats, linens, blankets and memorabilia were stored. I was allowed, weather permitting, to go up there to peruse the contents of the slanted roofed room. Too cold in the winter and too hot in the summer, the special times in the attic were spring and autumn. It was then that I climbed the narrow ladder to look into the garment bags, boxes, trunks, cabinets and cedar chests. There were lingering traces of moth balls and hints of the scent of Christmas evergreen.

This was a city of memory. Even if just from a season ago, the atmosphere instilled in me a reverence for beautiful visual detail. It was a neutral zone—the attic—a place to give memory a home and even offered me the feeling of a second chance.

In those early days on Corey Place, I had only my mind to create or recreate the events of my life. And this upstairs room was a fertile ground for the imagination. It was as if I could place my entire house in this one room and privately look closely at my story and the emotions that accompanied it. This place was a refuge. In it I forged a special relationship to things, awarding them a solid place in my foundation as permanent fixtures in the complexion of my spiritual longing. More than a room, the attic, with its army of treasures, was a salvation.

The Swimming Pool Hose

We had a swimming pool at the foot of our driveway on Corey Place in Spring Valley. It was a children's swimming pool in a dark green color. At the four corners were triangular metal seats, in the yellow color of our school patrol rain slickers. The pool would fill up like a full meal and sit there bulging in the heat inviting us to lounge in its cooling waters. The pool itself was about ten by ten feet. When we were young, we all fit into it at the same time. All of our neighbors had these pools, too. I liked the shape and size of ours the best. I especially enjoyed the swimming pool hose. We could use it with a nozzle to spray friends and family, in the spirit of play, or we could take the nozzle off to drink the water like an endless cocktail for a long hot summer's day.

The water from the swimming pool hose had a particular taste. Perhaps, it was the hint of the flavor of the rubber hose or the metallic bite of the nozzle. It was all the same water. They called Spring Valley by its name because of the many creeks, streams, and small rivulets of water that flowed through its borders. In later years, due to an emerging and long buried history of munitions testing and disposal of WWI chemical warfare agents, some called it Arsenic Valley, some called it Death Valley.

I wonder now, if that lazy afternoon drink contained any residue from the numerous chemical compounds used in the old testing laboratories, some of which were buried nearby, in some instances, hundreds of feet from where we sat in our cool green pool.

Perchlorate anyone?

Storybook Palaces

To anyone looking on, it seemed a typical urban landscape. For me, it was a labyrinth of imaginary outdoor rooms: ballrooms, dining salons, terraces, theatre stages, secluded gardens, boudoirs and dressing rooms. A leafy glade could provide the canopy for a bed—a parting between two bushes, an entrance to a clandestine garden—a clearing in the wood, a dance floor—a patch of green grass, a place to enact a tale—a circle of trees, a plot for a cottage in the deep woods. These outdoor rooms were the answer to an innermost private prayer for freedom. Here was a spot in the world of my own. Too young to build my own home, "Playing House" was the way forward.

I was fed by the beauty of my surroundings. I could drink its waters, bathe in the rain that fell upon it, languish in summer heat, spirit about in the lavender light of its springs, prance like a young horse in the blazing colors of its heady majestic falls and get lost in the beauty of its winter snows. My interior domains in this exterior world were crafted with great care.

It was in this atmosphere that friendships formed, stories were created, habits were learned, spirit increased, and I slowly and surely became inhabited by something alive from the earth below my feet. I suppose you could say this was normal, a gift to all children of any circumstance, if allowed free rein to the connection between their hearts and their young playful minds. But this was soul-seepingly different. It was as if I were somehow possessed by its aspect, wandering as a ghost, always with a question hovering: Why was this experience so transporting, so fully and all-consumingly mysterious? How did I come by this artistry, this way of seeing things deeply, layer by transparent layer? It seemed that this was magic bestowed.

This wizardry was left here long ago. It was a magic we were able to find all by ourselves, given the freedom of an era in which children were allowed to wander and explore. And so I acquired this magic. It was not under every step I took, but certainly some. It provided, for me, an underground framework that rendered me—over time—an actress.

Indian Burial Ground

Well . . .

This was just past the years of elegantly made Madame Alexander dolls, trading cards, paper dolls, and playing house. Wanting more adventure, I struck out into the distant yards, creeks, and forests of my neighborhood. Spring Valley was, and is, an urban forest, with rock formations and gardens, moss and Virginia Creeper and wild, on the ground, grape vines intrinsic to its topography.

Now, I was an explorer. I had a curiosity about what had preceded me, and I was drawn to the mystique of the Native Americans. I had read about them in my school lessons and I wondered if they had lived in the area. So naturally I set out with my friends to look for buried treasure.

One of the favorite spots was on a corner around the block from my first neighborhood residence. In the back of this house were a series of small rock gardens. We were given permission to go in to dig in this particular yard. In our quest for artifacts, we often unearthed bits of thick glass, some with sharp edges, and some old bottles. In so doing, we began our collections. We called this excavation site our Indian Burial Ground and were completely taken with what our unsuspecting hands brought out of the ground.

For our family, this was the last period of residency in Spring Valley, near the American University campus. The nature of play had changed, becoming more purposeful. Not all were interested. Some hung back to play dolls, dress up, board and card games. But for others, once these new directions had been found, there was no turning back.

Soon I left the territory of these first findings but continued digging in my new location. Lucky for me, or so I thought at the time, I now had a much larger backyard—on Sedgwick Street. The soil in my new yard, and in most of the yards on our new block, was of a dry, sandy consistency. There were areas of this material just outside of our back door, under the kitchen steps, along both sides of the house, under the willow trees, and under the wild full sprays of honeysuckle that draped the anchor fences of our yard. Opportunities for hunting were all around me.

What I did not realize at the time, and would have had no way of knowing, was that my neighborhood was to become the site of an ongoing investigation and munitions cleanup by the Army Corps of Engineers, and that the dirt and glass that I, routinely, handled as I grew up, " . . . may, or may not have been contaminated soil and discarded laboratory glass." These were materials that may have been utilized for the preparation and testing of poisonous gasses at the former American University Experiment Station (AUES) for use in chemical warfare in WWI, and subsequently buried in the ground beneath the yards of what became the homes in Spring Valley.

My family lived in two of these houses. The first was on Corey Place. The neighborhood garden, where we dug for our first treasure, is now a designated "Point of Interest" (POI). The second was on Sedgwick Street. This home was positioned two hundred feet from one of the circular testing trenches. The Sedgwick Trench. This street has reported many cases of disease, some of them rare, and in houses adjacent to one another.

What do I make of this in my own life? I find it to be an interesting layer of a story. I cannot change this, no matter what the outcome, and it is too late for blame. I can only raise my awareness, record my thoughts, and take the best care of myself that I can. The one thought that continues to rise to the surface is the truth of the experience that I had in these homes. With regard to that, I do wonder if the many dramatic and unusually numerous illnesses and emotional disturbances we experienced could have been a result of the indoor air we breathed, the water we drank and the soil that, daily, sifted through our hands. This will always be part of the puzzle, which I will try to piece together. For, at the end of the day, I remember, beyond a shadow of a doubt, what happened in those houses.

Spring Valley
Sedgwick
Street

Spring Valley — Sedgwick Street

Spring Valley—Sedgwick Street

Slow Dancing

It began in the early '60s. Elvis was crooning, "I Can't Help Falling in Love With You." The Lettermen were singing, "The Way You Look Tonight," "Smile," and "When I Fall in Love." Now, stages were set for church and community center dances. The popular songs became anthems. I knew all the words by heart and could whisper them to myself and hear them echoed by my partner as we sailed into each other's arms.

This time in my early teen years offered surprising moments of tenderness. The awakening was among the strongest and most romantic moments of my life. Permission was granted by the atmosphere to move in this new way. Suddenly, I was no longer a child. There was an awareness that was, at its root, simple. With nothing more to distract than the color of the room's floor or the chairs lining the walls, I, for the first time as I danced, could look all the way into another's eyes and find the reflection of the flickering candle of my soul. This was slow dancing.

Kissing in the Boiler Room

There was never anything quite this sexy. Remember? In those days there were parties in the homes of friends, usually, in basements that had been finished in knotty pine paneling. There would be a bar in the corner that would often be topped with a dwarf, a troll lamp or a lantern. These bars were mysterious wooden islands with glasses and bottles behind them. They represented a world I could not yet fathom. It was just there, in the golden lamp light, lurking as a promise of times to come.

Huh.

The precursors to these parties were church dances and early cotillions. These new occasions really served as smoke screens for what was then called "making out." This activity previewed during slow dances, then proceeded to the basement laundry room, where couples would hide behind the boiler to engage in romantic activities.

We were young, munching our potato chips and sipping Coca-Cola. We were reaching through the soft darkness for this new alluring feeling, and the exciting, slightly forbidden, behavior. Trying our wings, we embraced the delicious wild taste of this new flight—one that, through all of the years, no matter what came, would ever need to bow to its competition.

Now, when I go to Washington, DC, I ride the transit system as a senior citizen (something I never thought I would be). I pass by some of these houses where we had our initial brush with sexy dances and our first kisses. As tears fall from my eyes, it is not from sadness but gratitude for my life. If I do feel wistful, it is because I now feel invisible. I am at an age where most look beyond, not into my eyes. If they did look, they would see some of what we had during those quiet days with that great music, before all of the media, the screens, and the messages shared in the ether. They would see, captured, a picture of that one to one, no tech, old fashioned slow dancing and the incomparably sexy kissing in the boiler room.

The Trumpet

It just moved from house to house. It always had a place in a closet or finally, in later homes, up in the attic. It just kept climbing higher and higher, until it disappeared completely from view and from our minds. When it was still in the lower rooms, it lived mostly in my parents' bedroom closet. I would, from time to time, open the case, and stand, or sit, on a chair nearby to look at it with its gleaming brass, the mute, and the red velvet lining of its case. It was my father's trumpet.

Did he play the instrument? Do I even remember? Perhaps he did, once or twice. He liked the John Philip Sousa marches, the "Aïda Triumphal March," Ravel's Bolero and had a favorite album called *The Brave Bulls*. He liked the Glenn Miller Orchestra and the Ink Spots. He may have tried some of those melodies.

I am trying to remember how other music was played in our home. I think it was mainly from recordings. Maybe buying stereo equipment became a substitute for encouraging us to create our own sound. First there was the RCA Victor Victrola in the dining room with the thick 78, and later, 33rpm records. Then there was the triangular high fidelity unit in the living room. Then the TV/record player console, and the 45rpm record players in our children's rooms. Then, all of a sudden, there was a wall of sound with a mahogany box for each area of production. The speakers, the radio controls and dials, the reel to reel and the record player. This one unit, a Marantz 10B, made the journey all the way to the last family dwelling, and probably lasted because of the quality and because the initials on the speakers were JBL, those of my father: John Barry Letterman.

There were always the radio and the musical shows on the TV, but the mastery of an instrument, no. Only my sister took lessons. I did make an attempt later in life. Unfortunately, I never could concentrate adequately enough to learn.

I sometimes wonder what might have occurred if I had been given the time and encouragement to learn to play the piano or another instrument. I would have had something, at the very least, beyond staring at the unplayed trumpet in the closet. I just might have had a proficiency of my own.

Old Grand-Dad

This was not a relative or, as it turned out, even a friend. There was a breakfront in our dining room on Sedgwick Street. It had a central glass cabinet with drawers below, and two side cabinets also in glass. Below these were two narrow cabinets, with one shelf dividing their interiors. When I opened or closed these, I would hear a satisfying little click, not tinny or insubstantial, but solid, with a ping to it.

In the lower cabinet, on the left side, was a bottle of Old Grand-Dad whiskey. I think it held court there as a symbol. No one really drank it. The alcohol consumed in that house was either obvious, like lots and lots of cans of beer, or sherry, which was hidden in various spots: hat boxes, dresser drawers, the downstairs storage room, and sometimes the garage. This particular bottle of bourbon just sat there in the little side cabinet, at home on the dust free mahogany shelf, like a symbol of normality. "Here I am, dressed to kill, in amber, orange, gold and tawny brown, waiting for you!"

I think the myth may have been—If the vessel remained full and still resting in place, no one was drunk, violent or fighting. This was a house where there was polite, moderate, social drinking. But in the background, if someone were to want a little something extra. Old Grand-Dad would be standing, at attention, a sentry nearby.

I don't believe anyone was fooled by this.

Cleaning the House

The ritual of cleaning in our house was a top to bottom affair, it was not just cleaning, it was my job. It was riding the wild surf of fear and broken-heartedness. To this day, I can remember every corner of every surface and architectural shape, from the insides of closets, to the construction of individual pieces of furniture. Not one grain of salt would be left on a piece of shelf paper, not a crumb left on a counter's surface. This was boot camp!

Cleaning cleared a path through the curtain of worries that hovered over my head. There was no need for household products because the home was spotless to begin with. This was an obsessive-compulsive, room by room, closet by closet task. It involved straightening, aligning, checking and organizing every domestic detail, from the wrinkles, that might have been left in an already made up bed, to a shoe hanging at a slightly crooked angle in a caddy, to a dress or a suit askew on a hanger. Not a trickle of water, not a trace of tooth powder or paste would be acceptable. Attention! All must be in perfect order.

Somewhere along the line, cleaning became a way to cope, then a ritual, then almost a meditation. Finally, it became my way of life. Step by step, gesture by gesture, each minute became an opportunity for the administration of care. As if, in applying myself to the needs of people and my interiors, a way forward would be revealed, leading me, once and forever, home.

The Makers of the Americas

I was in my early teens, and by now beginning to withdraw from an addiction to amphetamines: Benzedrine, Dexedrine and Dexamyl. These had been prescribed by my pediatrician at the suggestion of my parents as diet and productivity aids when I was 9 years old. The goal was for me to excel in school, be bone thin, and manage my adult household duties on Sedgwick Street in Spring Valley, in Northwest Washington, DC. When no longer permitted to take the pills (which I did not want in the first place) things fell apart and were difficult for me. This was especially true of homework. I had a secret problem with learning. It had always been a strain to concentrate and retain information and now, without the assistance of the "diet pills," it was even more challenging. While performing my high wire act on speed, anything had been possible—and no one noticed. No one knew what I was hiding. I was ashamed of myself for these limitations.

Eventually, I was found out. My textbook for Early American History was a book entitled, *The Makers of the Americas*. It was beige, with a spine of melon orange and black line drawings of explorers on the front cover, filled in with a light aqua tint. The look of the cover I could recount in detail, the inside material was another matter altogether.

On one particular evening my father instructed me to read a chapter, informing me that he would quiz me on the contents in one hour. At the end of my study period he reappeared, perused a paragraph or two from the assignment and queried, "Who was Balboa?" Silence. He repeated the question, now very angry with me, "Who was Balboa?" I couldn't tell him. I just did not know. I am not sure, even today, if I really know who he was.

What I do remember is, that for this learning misdemeanor, I was removed to my parent's room across the hall, and beaten until red welts formed on my backside. This was not an uncommon practice in those days.

I was so afraid of this particular failure, and my own sense of growing shame, that I became, overnight, a scholar. My tool for academic achievement was a raging, ragged fear. I studied and studied and studied, and then . . . I waited with held breath to be dropped from the class rosters. Right up until the moment of my graduation from high school, I felt like an imposter.

In reality, I had flown by the seat of my pants and landed with my feet on the ground like the others. I would not—until much later—know how to honor, and accept, my style of learning. I did learn to do my best, not to attempt perfection, but to give myself over to the romance of study itself.

In so doing, my creative style was born. It is a style whose roots are in significant pain, but which has learned to embrace joy and to celebrate humanity, while cultivating a work ethic and learning to survive.

Old Spice

He was lost to me, my Father. I just couldn't find him. Sometimes, I would go into his bathroom and pick up his bottle of Old Spice aftershave. It was smooth glass in an off-white color, beige almost, with a sailing vessel depicted on the front. The top was crowned with a silver metal collar. Into the opening fit a tiny ridged stopper that I would remove to peer inside, as if, in straining to see into the bottle, I would find him.

Well . . .

He wasn't there, but what happened next made it seem as if he were. For in taking out the little stopper, the scent of my father would come to me. It was second best, but this was evocative of one who seemed to have abandoned ship.

I would see him then, fresh in his suit, ready for a day's work at the Federal Communications Commission in the Old Post Office building in downtown DC on 12th and Pennsylvania Avenue. He would be wearing that unusual sweet but decidedly masculine fragrance, one that seemed to say to the wearer:

> *Be of good faith, son.*
> *You have what it takes.*
> *Go out then, to meet the world.*
> *Try not to worry so. Try not to be afraid.*
> *Your children will be all right.*
> *Your wife loves you, and will forgive you.*
> *You are young, still.*
> *You have time.*

You are not a bad man, John, just one who may,
from time to time, be overwhelmed, and troubled by,
the weight of the world and the many responsibilities
placed upon your young shoulders.

> *Others may not understand you, but I do.*
> *I will envelop you in this scent to guide and to protect you.*
> *I am your signature and your companion.*
> *And so, you are not alone.*

In a moment such as this, privately, quietly, almost reverently, I would place the tiny stopper in its circular home. Over the years of turmoil I grew to understand, but continued to miss, a real connection to my father.

So . . .

I would often come back to this room, to the little sailing ship that carried him through the rough waters of his life, and then I would gently remove the tiny top to inhale the scent of his saving grace.

The Maids

These were the women who, one by one, witnessed the entire story. These were the individuals who ushered us through our early lives. They arrived at the bus stops from what must have been far away places. Upon reaching our house, they filled it with a love and care that rescued all of us. They are all gone now, this parade of wonderful women, who were mothers to our family. They were each unique and beloved.

These were the pilgrims who gave me courage on my own pathway, my unusual journey, taken on buses, trains, and long walks. I feel, on my path, only a fraction of what they must have endured, by doing what it took to find their ways home. These women came to us in any kind of weather. They worked because they had to. This was their life, their employment. No matter how cold, hot, muddy, or clear it was, they showed up. They worked tirelessly, creating order as they set about their endless tasks in the cleaning of our house: polishing the silver, doing the laundry, ironing the clothes, making the beds, pressing the linens, and preparing the food.

They calmly urged us to a better place. What they probably did not count on was that they would be called upon to accompany us on such a turbulent ride. In possession of their own trials and heartbreak, they were asked to bear ours as well. In their way, they glued us back together. Maybe it was the strength of their beliefs and their faith in God that did it. These came with them when they entered our home with their beauty and their healing. I always held on to the hope that when these women were present, things might be less dramatic, less scary, and less volatile.

Looking back now, I do not know how, with the elements, and in those troubled times, they marshaled the bravery to travel those distances, and do all that very hard work. They taught us to endure the unbearable, setting an example with their own template of strength.

These were angels in uniform. They arrived daily, through the years, beautiful African-American women, to don their dove-grey dresses with cotton and organdy aprons and were a blessing to us all. The turmoil in our house was not unique, but mercifully, neither was the grace ministered by these women in their humility and elegance.

The Evening Dress

There is always one gown that stands out. This one belonged to my mother. It was a '60s design fashioned of a brown, white, and pale yellow silk over skirt. Under this, emerging from the front in a full graduated ruffle, was a pale lemon underskirt of tulle. There were 30 rows of this material falling in a cascade of beauty to a graceful ballet length. It was cinched at the waist with a golden brown velvet band. The bodice was of the same material as the skirt. The garment was fitted with a v-neck and had arms that were cut in a bit past the line of the shoulder. All over the dress was a constellation of tiny rhinestones in the fabric and a hue of violet, of which we could never guess the origin. It was a masterpiece, this dress. My mother was still a beautiful woman and she wore it to perfection.

The Blue Closet

The blue closet was actually green. It just felt blue. It was in the attic room at the top of the stairs on the third floor of our home on Sedgwick Street in Spring Valley, in Northwest Washington, DC.

The room was small, with two windows, one in a corner alcove overlooking the backyard and the weeping willow trees, the other in the wall facing the side yard. This room belonged to my baby brother Danny.

The closet was in the southeast corner of the room. It was fairly deep and had one slanted ceiling wall.

The time period felt like the beginning of the end. The prelude to the exiles and the premature emotional burials. In this closet were the remnants of my mother's dreams and signals marking the end of my own. I was 12 years old. These "remnants" were the party dresses and the evening gowns. I would go up there when no one was home or when my mother was "sleeping," and sit in the stifling humidity under the gowns.

Some of the skirts were so wide that if there was a breeze from the window fan, or even from my own exhalations, they would peal over me like bells. Church bells, sleigh bells, school bells, dinner bells, Hell's bells. I would hide under these swaying fabrics—the nets and chiffons— and will myself to disappear to a room where once I felt safe. I would recall the old pink wall paper with the swirling, iridescent baby blue and pearly white bubbles, pray they would rescue me, float forever and not burst apart. When I retired from my afternoon reveries, it would often be in "the blue hour" and time for me to return to the duties of the house.

This would also be the moment when these old gowns would wait to report for their evening out. Alas! No one came for them anymore. My parents, were not, as it turns out, a desirable 'life of the party,' and were no longer invited—anywhere. And so it was, these dresses remained in their places in the blue closet.

I would go then, as in a trance, to my tasks, and would I swear I could hear the dresses sighing, plaintively calling to me, their only remaining friend.

Time to Get Up!

For a window of time in the early '60s, my mother would take amphetamines to keep going. This began after the death of her father. At that time, something in my mother, already at risk from the effects of continuous domestic unease, changed. This was the turning point. It was then that the real trouble began.

She was wired up for sound and down for the count all at the same time. I, to the degree that I was able to, took over. I even cooked (I do not cook now). This was during the Teem, Tang, Wonder Bread, Velveeta, Spam, and creamed scalloped potatoes period. This was the rotary dial, iron all of the shirts and bed linens, and push button Highpoint Range, Betty Crocker cookbook period. For me, it was the last of the chubby-tubby time, and the beginning of my roller coaster ride to Good Housekeeping teenage slenderness. This was the pre-thin get off the merry-go-round, yo-yo, eating-of-the-entire-chocolate-mint-cookie shipment from the Girl Scouts period.

In the evening, fat, tired and frightened, I would go to the island of safety, which I found in my bedroom, and try to sleep. Finally, after all of the chores and the homework and the care of small children, I would try to get some rest.

It was then, in the small hours of the night, while I looked for respite, that my mother would come alive. She would, brightly lit like a holiday tree, begin her work by starting to operate all of the machines in the house. Now, it was time to turn on the lights and lamps, run the dishwasher and the vacuum, do the wash, use the dryer, wax the basement floors, whip up a batch of batter for morning pancakes in the blender, and to clean the windows with the tiny squeaking noise that matched her crying and her midnight-and-beyond self-chatter.

Sometimes, if I was lucky—and I stayed on red alert for luck—Dad would be passed out cold from drinking, snoring away in the night. Sometimes, if I was not so fortunate, I would hear the snoring stop. Then, as his heavy feet hit the floor, the wood would thrum with the vibration of his uncontrollable anger. It would be then that the bedroom door would open to crash and splinter in his wake and he would storm down the stairs of our home on Sedgwick Street to confront my mother.

In the basement there was a small windowless room of knotty pine wood. For us it served as a storage area and was the place where we played and where the Christmas presents were wrapped. In the middle of the room was a support beam of black iron about five inches around that went from the floor to the ceiling.

Now, bolting down the basement steps, my father would go into this room and commence banging on the pole with a crow bar or a hammer, waking the house up like a fire-alarm, yelling at the top of his lungs, "Time to Get Up!"

Now, mother would attempt to stop him. The babies would begin to cry, and the rest of us who had heard, would run from bed to get in the middle of their fighting. My mother, now frightened and furious, would run away to start another machine—the automobile. She would back the car out of the garage and would leave us gaping in terror as she careened onto the street, speeding away at three o'clock in the morning.

We would now begin our vigil hoping for the resumed sounds of snoring above, and for those of a car coming back into the driveway. Only when the garage door closed could we return to our rooms. It would then be all quiet on the Northwestern Washington DC front . . . until the following night.

Quit Being So Dramatic

It was a plea, really, that I made to my father that night. I can still feel it—the pain—and the deep sorrow and humiliation of it.

I was in my room on Sedgwick Street. I was wearing my new long pink nightgown with little blue flowers. It had a matching robe, which I had set aside. I was getting ready for bed.

My parents were both active alcoholics. My father routinely came home drunk. My mother stayed drunk during the day and was usually high on pills at night. One evening, before the cycle of insanity featuring her tour-de-force electric cleaning of the house until the wee hours of the morning was about to start, I asked to speak with my father as he seemed not to be as drunk or as angry as usual.

I thought that it would be a good time to speak of my feelings. I had been put in charge of almost everything that was not being done by our domestic help, our visiting Grandmother, or occasionally, fitfully, by my mother. It was an exhausting and frightening time. I asked for an audience with my father because I thought he might be able to help me.

I probably said something like 'Dad, the situation here is very hard. Emotionally, I feel that I cannot take it anymore.' It was something like that—probably a bit expanded—but still brief. I began to weep. Essentially, this was a cry for help. He looked at me, with his face now raised to a scarlet boiling point, drew back his fist, and socked me in the left breast, saying, "Quit being so Dramatic!"

My little preteen frame caved at the impact.

I never asked for his help again.

I did, however, go into the theatre.

Snow

The snows that fell between 1948, when I was born, and 1963, when our family left the environs of Spring Valley in Northwest Washington, DC seemed different from the ones that fell in later years. In those days, it fell hard, heavy and thick. Covering the ground, it gleamed like shattered glass in the sun. On overcast or still, snowy days, it glimmered in the dark, as if to wink at us.

I never understood the difference. Something was odd, off, not quite right.

I had the same sensation when I went for neighborhood sledding at American University. Our preferred hill descended a large, long slope at the base of the administrative buildings and classrooms, which were just below and stage left of the old WMAL radio tower, our own highly anticipated beacon to the North Pole.

We would assemble in our places on the top of the giant hill and prepare to go down, fearless on our flexible flyers, or in our aluminum saucers to go over ski jumps fashioned of ice, mid-slope. We would fly down on our sleds or soar like silver birds over the jumps until we landed again, face to face, with that gleaming, crystalline snow, which, in the aftermath of our rides, we would eat, body and soul. The light in it lured us. We would sit, freezing, huddled in our winter bundles and, in gales of laughter, feast on its blinding bounty.

What we did not realize at the time, was that the soil beneath our icy fingers was "in all probability" filled with the residue from experiments made in the WWI testing laboratories on this site at the former American University Experimental Station. But somehow, we did know, even then in the dark, there was some mystery in the air. We knew this was our special snow.

Well . . .

I recently went on a guided tour of the American University Campus where I learned some of the details of this history, and another piece of the puzzle of my life fell into place. I went looking for my hill. Now, 60 plus years later, what had been almost a mountain, was gone. Excavated, examined, carried away? Another puzzle.

As I look back on these large hills and the smaller scale gentle residential lawns, I wonder:

Could this have been the past bleeding through the earth to command our focus, to capture our attention? Was it carving inscriptions into the shiny carpets of white that lay below our windows and on our sleigh hills?

Like letters to future friends?

Saying, perchance

> *I am here under you*
> *silent, perhaps*
> *but*
> *still here*
>
> *I am in your water*
> *your earth*
> *the cold powder beneath your feet*
>
> *I am in the air*
> *in your garden*
> *and in your house*
>
> *I am your bright glittering madness*
> *if you could but hear me*
> *I am calling you, teaching you*
> *warning you*
>
> *Tomorrow I will melt*
> *but I will return*
> *perhaps, not again, in the aura of this precipitation*
> *but, I will come back to you*
>
> *For you are sliding down my arms on this hill*
> *but you are living on my grave in the*
> *5000 block of Sedgwick Street*

Black-Eyed Pea Soup

On New Year's Day, our tradition was to prepare a large pot of black-eyed pea soup. This was for good luck. I never liked the soup. Although a good old family recipe was used, it did not appeal to me. I was, and still am, a mashed potato and gravy girl. The tradition of making the soup and serving it was another story, and one that had comforted me through the years.

The last year of observing this custom in our family on Sedgwick Street, that I can recall, was in the early '60s, in a year when the holiday fell on a Sunday.

At this time, our family was steeped in constant unhappiness and turmoil. My mother was alternately passed out from drinking or high on pills. My father was in the throes of alcoholism and had terrible bouts of rage. This anger was directed towards all of us, especially my mother.

That particular Sunday, I was in the kitchen watching the soup simmer on the range. I was, also, as was my custom, setting the table in the breakfast room. I had already cleaned everything in sight and was strangely apprehensive about the coming celebration.

Since the morning, my parents had been at odds, simmering, like the soup. Despite the tension, we were trying to maintain the illusion of a family, and we still dined together. There were seven of us: three older children and two very young ones, one of those in a high chair.

So there we were in the breakfast room in our house on Sedgwick Street. This was a small welcoming room off of the kitchen. It had the same black and white tile as the kitchen except these tiles were larger. We ate at a round table that might have also been a poker table. It had a round leather cover that folded in sections. I set the table and brought in the seat for my baby sister. The atmosphere was all ready for a happy holiday occasion.

When it was time to gather for our traditional meal, my mother was already drunk. My father was drinking and very, very angry. We assembled around the circular table. I prayed we would make it through the meal. The good luck dinner did not last long. The volatile combination of moods were not conducive to either luck or peace. My father became increasingly angry at something that was said and with one motion of his hand pulled the table cloth and sent the now-full bowls of hot celebration soup flying through the air to the floor. With everyone screaming and crying and fleeing the scene, my attempts to move the young children to safety are what I remember.

Now the scene was different. The dishes, and the soup, and the table service covered the floor with a river of liquid, broken china, and glassware. The pieces were everywhere in the room, even falling down the stairs to the finished basement below. I spent the next two hours alone, panicked, crying, and afraid. I cleaned up the mess until, in the end, I stood on the black and white tiles, now free of soup and glass, in splashes of bright red.

This was the last year we were to spend in our house on Sedgwick Street, a house that was strong, solid, graceful and elegant, but one that from the moment we took up residence, rendered us, one and all: mad as hatters.

The Butter Sandwiches

No wonder I gained weight. In 1962, wiped out from the stiflingly humid weather of a DC summer's afternoon, I would look for relief in the form of a snack. This would, more often than not, be a cool glass of orange Tang or Kool-Aid offered in a variety of colorfully packaged powdery flavors. Either or both were poured from a patterned glass pitcher filled with ice cubes. As an accompaniment to the refreshing drinks, I would prepare a sandwich in an open-faced style. The ingredients were two pieces of Wonder Bread, which would be retrieved from pillow soft packages with red, yellow, and blue dots, and then placed on the formica counter. Immediately butter was spread in a thick carpet. When this was done, I would dust the surface with a generous portion of granulated sugar. Upon completion of this recipe, I would run with the orange, white, and yellow meal to the screened-in porch, to a shaded spot under the weeping willows in the yard, or to the back kitchen steps to enjoy it.

As I recall the butter sandwich period of my life took place right before the bitter end of baby fat and preteen weight. I have not had a butter sandwich in years, but I still have a generous portion of figure.

Looking at Houses

I think that it started about the time we lost our hold on the family Tourist Home and found we were going to move from Spring Valley. Why we needed to leave a house that was paid for, in an elegant location like this, was beyond my comprehension. In the end, it may have saved our lives. The jury is still out.

The fact remains that in 1963 we started, as a family, every Sunday, to go looking at houses. This would involve traveling to view "model homes" my father found for us in the newspaper.

We all needed an escape. We had been trained to admire and seek out beauty in a house and to appreciate impressive, solid building materials and designs. Even young, we were a discerning audience. Every Sunday, like clockwork, once this routine began, we set forth on a trek to look for a new domain. I hoped this would offer us a fresh start and a chance to improve our circumstances. We went to various suburban developments to look at these models. In the end, I discovered that I was spoiled. Although what we saw was of a high standard, nothing could compare to the design and construction of the WC&AN Miller homes I had lived in thus far. Any purchase in one of these new neighborhoods would last for a year or two, but we would always move back to the familiar ambiance, detail, and the style of quality that we had left behind. Our foundation became forever cemented in this taste.

In the meantime, a new habit took hold, one that promised that a new location could offer a solution to mend the hole in my heart. Long after we no longer searched these model homes as a Sunday pastime, I held onto this yearning and told myself that my emotional distress could be "fixed up" by anything from an antebellum mansion in the South, to a handy man special in a decrepit town. Not to mention, the promise of attractive workmen, but that is a different book.

The notion of an unfolding day had long called me to be a guest in its slow embrace. What seems to have eluded me is a place to rest and call home. I explained to a friend once that I root as does the strawberry vine—along a lengthy, often winding path. My friend offered that I might consider repotting the plant.

I really do now wish to place my feet on the earth in one spot, so I have a sense of sanctuary, solidity, and security. A feeling of safety that, in my family, was absent, leaving me wandering from house to house to house, and place to place to place, looking for what I was missing.

A Little Birdie Told Me

I looked forward to signs of Spring from my bedroom window on Sedgwick Street. My room was on the second floor, the first door on the left at the top of the stairs. It was a room painted pink with a pink, black, and white tiled bathroom. It had a shower stall that I was certain had a bear hiding in it.

Winter was lovely in those days, with its moist snow falls, long walks out-of-doors, and snowmen populating the yards. But, like all winters, at a certain moment, it is time for it to be over. It seemed to me that each year, all of a sudden, one day I would wake up to a warmer light coming through the windows.

I used to have a wide wing-backed chair with multi-colored upholstery in a whimsical rooster print. I would curl up in this chair and listen to the bird song, and as spring advanced, the sound of the tree saws of the industrious landscape workers who prepared the gardens and yards for the warmer seasons.

Spring's arrival was refreshing. The universe of my little room opened and I prepared to go out into the world to hatch the plans I had made during the months of hibernation. We had beautiful side gardens and a large backyard, so I did not have far to go to bring these plans to life. In the early years in this home, I felt heavy and anxious. I was always full, but empty of an idea of where I should run to, except, under the covers to dream, to school, to Atlantic City in the summer, to the Tourist Home, or outside to the shelter of the beauty that was our neighborhood.

Even then, the wild winds of change were blowing and the mysteriousness of my childhood was being set in stone. In that one house, more than any other, I felt that the seeds were planted for who I would become. And when, in the early spring, I heard nature's song, a light note entered my story. This one, unlike the darker melody of our house, was sweet. It seemed a message from somewhere, that someday, no matter what happened, I would find my way.

In this house, I felt as if I were being put to sleep. As if, like Sleeping Beauty, I had a spell set upon me which could only be broken with love's kiss. And now, many, many years later, I feel that I have been kissed by love. How do I know this? I know, because, newly awakened, I hear through my windows a fresh song, a kiss of new life and spring.

I know, because a little birdie told me.

Old Farm
Spring Hill

Old Farm—Spring Hill

Old Farm — Spring Hill

The Pink Pants and the Pink Sweater

These garments were cheap, but I was thin, and when you are THIN, even cheap clothes look good. The outfits were not the main event. Front and center, it was the atmosphere in which they were found. This was at the new Super Giant in the Westwood Shopping Center. Now that we were no longer living near to our favorite GC Murphy & Company, this became a new destination for family shopping.

The Super Giant and neighboring Drug Fair offered a preview of retail times moving forward, featuring a modernized grocery and drug store experience. There were brighter fluorescent lights, wider aisles, more departments, merchandise with less charm, and foods presented to be more interesting and healthy than they actually were. The layouts were grandiose and tiresome. But, there was one great thing. The Super Giant was the evening place of employment for my former Junior High School science teacher. He worked as a checker in the evenings and had been my first romantic fantasy crush.

I was still completely infatuated with this man. Because of this, I had embraced my junior high school science project with a stylish vigor and abandon. I never imagined that diagramming the composition of eight elements could be so exciting. Suddenly the properties of Zinc, Iron, Copper, Nickel, Aluminum, Tin, Uranium and Titanium became extremely important to me.

One evening, when I was in the frozen foods section of the new super store, while my mother did the household shopping, I felt that I needed a diversion. It was at this time that I discovered the fashion department. This featured rack after rack of ordinary clothing. I was delighted with the distraction this provided. While my mother shopped, I browsed, waiting for a glimpse of my new friend, planning ahead to pretend surprise, if I saw him.

Although the pink pants and little matching sweater top I found on the rack at the Super Giant were without expensive fashion appeal, I loved them far more than my outfits from the formal stores downtown on F Street. After all, they were chosen by a 23-inch-waisted young teenager, in love, waiting in line to be "checked out" by the object of her affection.

Mount Vernon Seminary

It was very clear the days of our public high school experience were at an end. I attended Gordon Junior High School in the Georgetown vicinity near Glover Park on Wisconsin Avenue. This was a good school with an eccentric, but well-prepared, faculty. It was also a beautiful old facility. In the 1960s in Washington, DC significant racial tension began to erupt in the community, finding its way into the schools. With these undercurrents surfacing in our academic hallways, a decision was made to send me to private school.

The institution chosen for me was Mount Vernon Seminary. This was a preparatory private school for young women and was located within the district on Foxhall Road. My closest girlfriend from those earlier years, who had been a schoolmate at Gordon Junior High, applied for admission as well. We were both accepted and began making arrangements to start our years there.

This was the big pocketbook, girl–boy crush, Aqua Net hair spray, transistor radio period. It was a time of experimentation and some willfulness. We needed the guidance and direction the larger public school was not able to, nor inclined, to offer. I believe the turning point for my parents came when I poured a bottle of peroxide on the front of my beautiful brown hair in an effort to streak it. It dribbled haphazardly down the back of my head to create a stripe of light color. So there I was, wearing a black wool dress with a white collar for my first meeting with the headmistress in Post Hall, and I looked like a skunk in a pilgrim costume. I do think, as they regarded me with raised brows, they hoped collectively this look would change, and soon, under the new influences I would encounter.

I will admit, there was a certain *je ne sais quoi* that differentiated the clean swept old junior high school halls and the sumptuous, but understated old world charm of the reception hall I entered that afternoon at my new private school.

At Gordon, there had been an air of permissiveness, mostly because our numbers were too many for our trials and dawning behaviors to be noticed. At Mount Vernon, there was a quietude where one could hear every footfall and take note of every gesture of our first moments. Mount Vernon Seminary was a gated facility with sloping drives and lamplit walkways leading to the residences of the prep school and the long-ago established junior college. The pathways through the campus were wide enough to offer the impression of space which encouraged intellectual and social exchange between and after classes. One thing was clear. This was a chance to reach for something new. No one was going to do it for any of us. We had, each of us, to make an effort.

The student body was made up of day students from the area and the boarders who came from the eastern states, with a concentration of individuals from Georgia, North and South Carolina, and Virginia. This was a moment of privilege and I realized I needed to take it seriously. This open door afforded all of us an opportunity for healthy competitiveness. It was here, by accident or by design, that I summoned the focus to cement a serious approach to study. This came as a gift, a by-product of this rare education and expert teaching. I was lucky to be there. The Seminary was in its last years of existence. I had already lost so much else. Beloved neighborhoods, vacation destinations, and our Tourist Home, soon to be demolished. I was not about to lose this as well.

This was the place where I learned to excel. It was also here that I enjoyed my five minutes of beauty. Here, that I drove a car to school with my homework placed carefully on the black bucket seat of my prized maroon Chevrolet Corvair Monza. With the popular songs of the '60s playing on the radio, this car took its place beside other Corvairs, GTOs, Mustangs, Impalas, Malibus, Bonnevilles, Oldsmobiles, Lincoln Continentals, and the MG convertible.

Although I did not feel that I fit in at the beginning, there was something intangible that provided a way forward for me. I know this began with that afternoon in Post Hall on the graceful campus of Mount Vernon Seminary, a place that had fostered and made whole the dreams of many young women over the years, and was now making a way for mine.

The British Invasion and the Funk

Well . . .

It might as well have been an air raid, the way it got our attention. Not since Sputnik and the Bay of Pigs was there such an uproar. Now I realize, as I think back on it, everything was about to change.

Enter James Brown, The Beatles, The Rolling Stones, The Yardbirds —but as a friend of mine says, "Let me back up."

James Brown—now, let's not forget, I was living in Washington, DC. This was the capital city, and this was funk. I remember seeing this fabulous performer with the Flames at the Howard Theatre in the mid '60s. I felt like I had been introduced to the Godfather of Soul.

Time stood still when these musical artists entered the picture. We all had to adjust our thinking. Our world had tilted on its axis. This music put a face to what was beating at our core. For those of us who heard the sounds from the beginning, it felt like it would be enough energy and inspiring sound to light a fire under a lifetime of creativity and personal style. Some of us had the courage to ride this wild horse, others buried the awareness alive, allowing themselves to be tossed about by its potency, not understanding how to deal with the feelings and the new knowledge it brought. No less powerful, but easier somehow to incorporate, were the sounds of the Beatles and the Rolling Stones. This was not precisely cerebral, but for me, it was more in the thinking than, immediately and viscerally, in the body.

Caught by the tide the sound brought, even my mother would race to the little record store on Wisconsin Avenue for a new Beatles 45 rpm. "She Loves You" had arrived—Yeah, yeah, yeah. We were both still reeling from "I Wanna Hold Your Hand." If smoke had indeed been in our eyes as the decade began, it was now in our eyes, our hearts our bodies and our souls. We knew the words to all these songs. We heard them on 45 and 33 rpm turntables and on the radio in the car.

It was everything to me. It now underscored my homework, my drive to be thin, my dating, my future planning, my home life, and my relations with family members and friends. This was when music, always there in my life, took over.

Not until the '70s double *White Album* and George Harrison's stunning "All Things Must Pass" did it begin to diminish, and then, it was only because everything in the world around us had shifted. In some ways, it was too late, because, by then, it was in us. Right along with the hot flaming songs of James Brown, we were branded. This music arrived at a moment of profound change in history, lifestyle, and social integration and, it was everywhere.

In Washington, DC where R&B was already like a heart beat, we took music into our bones, and now added to this soulful rhythm a new atmosphere of romance. The way was shown to us by Motown, an undulating breeze blown across funk. We did not miss a word or skip a beat.

The sounds and words came at a time of pain and suffering for throngs of people who had seen no way forward until now—the music pulled us together like a lullaby offering a distant promise of accord. It came right out of Detroit to our front doors and onto the machines that spun our vinyl platters round and round, turning us upside down.

The White Bathing Suit

It did not really take that long. It never does. What it does require is a decision. Okay! So, I decided. I had heard them call me 'fatty' enough. I was so uncomfortable. I felt so sad. I had just had it with my weight going up and down.

Those were the days of the Metrecal diet drink, but not for me. I think I just stopped eating entirely or took in only enough to get by.

It was then that I found the white two-piece bathing suit. It was nothing special, but I knew I had to be thin to wear it. I knew what the solution was. One Tab soft drink, or two. Or, one Tab soft drink, and one True-Aid orange drink complemented with a package of Newport cigarettes.

If I went to the Old Farm neighborhood pool, and had not eaten that day, I would allow myself to have one Moon Pie from the vending machine, but I would need immediately to do ten laps in the pool and there would be NO DINNER! And so it went, my home run to slenderness. I took center stage in my white bathing suit and brought it home to the plate.

Of course, there is always something waiting when one problem is solved, and men were waiting for me. They were available in all shapes and sizes. West Point cadets, military school boys, private school smarties, fast public high school Romeos, rich ones, poor ones—not too many of those, handsome devils and winsome shy youths. This was a veritable Whitman Sampler . . . You could pick one from each category or specialize, if you preferred. They drove Karmann Ghia's, Malibu Super Sports, GTO'S, Chrysler New Yorkers, trucks, Cadillacs, and VW Bug Convertibles. Heck! They could have pulled up in a June Bug and I would have hopped right in. I didn't go for the motorcycles or the Metrecal, but these boys had talent. I became an avid and willing apprentice. From the swimming pool, it was a short hop to the dating pool and I came at it from the high dive.

The Beach Boys were singing "Don't Worry Baby" and I didn't. That is, until it was too late to save my dignity or restore my reputation. It all went up in smoke and three bases in the back and front seats of their cars in the 1960s.

I was a beautiful young girl in a white bathing suit, hot as the sun, kissing a pristine future goodbye. I was, in the end, way off base. My diet and subsequent new hunger left me thin as a rail, walking the plank.

The Pink Suit

This was the suit I wore when I was a size sub-zero. I was now trim, trim, trim, with a 22" waist and an attitude to match. The suit had a tight, just-below-the-knee-length skirt, and a silk paisley blouse with pink, purple, and black designs on a white background.

Completing the ensemble was a short, pink, elbow length jacket with a lining to match the blouse. This was my inaugural test suit. I could never eat a full meal for fear that, at the end of it, the suit would not fit.

This was the true beginning of a new, almost obsessive, drive to be even thinner than I had become in the aftermath of the white bathing suit, Tab cola, Newport cigarette, Moon Pie, no dinner diet. I wanted to carve myself out of my skin to look like a statue. No longer on diet pills, I turned to laxative abuse and weighing myself. I would hang on to my many-squared enamel vanity in the bathroom, which I kept polished to a high glossy sheen, while placing my feet on the scale. The goal was to be NO MORE THAN 115 pounds. If I had my hand on the counter and lifted up slowly, I could see that I really weighed 111-112. I was like a marionette on strings bobbing up and down to find my image in the mirror. With each view, I hoped to appear slimmer and slimmer. I was able to wear the pink suit for about two years until I forced myself to move beyond its confines to other test garments.

Thus I laid to rest the threadbare pieces of my treasured ensemble. The new challenging rack of clothes waiting for the routine was well in place. This was a graduation. Now, as I tried all the clothing on, the accompanying fashion parade was augmented by grueling sets of exercises, chosen to ensure visual success in any outfit, in every mirror on the wall.

My pink suit was like a warm up drill. The Grey Suit became a trophy for the exhibition of my thinness in public.

The Grey Suit

I had arrived. I had been chosen as a cheerleader and I was absolutely terrible. I could fit into the outfit and was, surprisingly to everyone, attractive. The sad second half of the tale was that I never could learn the cheers and was not even remotely athletic. I was, in any case, thin and very gratified to have been chosen. I had been out of shape and passed over for anything of this nature for as long as I could remember.

About the same time, I was selected to model in our high school fashion show. This was scheduled to take place in the Lafayette Hotel near Farragut Square in DC. The hotel was owned by the father of a classmate.

Now, this was incredible! There were twelve models picked from our class. One afternoon we were taken to a French boutique in the Friendship Heights area of the city. Every article of clothing which I tried on fit me. We each had five garments to model, and we all wore an evening gown in the finale. Mine was a white satin dress with an empire waist. The bodice was made of a shimmering, jewel toned brocade with a pink border. It was a stunning creation. But the article of clothing I remember most was: The Grey Suit.

This was fashioned in three pieces. It was made of a very fine, thin wool in a medium grey color. The fitted suit jacket had a lemon silk lining and two mother-of-pearl buttons for closure. The skirt was cut to a silhouette somewhere between A-line and straight, and fell just below the knee. The under blouse was of the same fabric as the skirt and the jacket but was printed with small white polka dots on the grey background. It was fitted with a row of buttons down the back. The neckline was scooped with a ruffled collar. It was a very feminine design and suited me perfectly.

My hair was styled in the chin-length cut that was always best for my face and height.

I will never forget this gorgeous suit. At the close of the fashion show, we were allowed to keep one garment. This was the one I chose. For me, it was a symbol that I was finally fitting in, that I, after all, had the right qualifications. It was as if I had won a prize for losing all of that weight. Like its predecessor, the Pink Suit, I tried this one on daily to measure my size and, now, my place in the world.

To this day, I do not know what became of the Grey Suit. Probably during a period when I held disdain for my past and privilege, I threw it in some trash bin or other.

I might be able to find a suit as lovely as this one again. But I will never be able to duplicate the feeling of wearing a beautiful, form-fitting, French garment in a high school fashion show.

The Green Velvet Dress

I was going along with the required preparatory school uniforms with the benefit of sometimes being permitted to wear street clothes or party dresses to designated functions. I viewed these events as liberating. It was in these arenas that I began to exhibit a young adult fashion sense. I was still wearing the handmade clothing my Grandmother created for me with a peppering of an occasional ensemble from Julius Garfinckel's, Woodward and Lothrop, or Jelliffs.

During these evenings out, time seemed to divide itself in half, as youth gave way to adulthood. This came quietly, quickly and unexpectedly. One evening during this period, our class president, and friend, seemed to be the one who moved the clock forward for all of us. She was one of the more accomplished and focused in our midst. Poised and smart, she had an empathic spirit that was comforting to be around. She was also beautiful and dressed in carefully selected, pretty, if slightly conservative garments for our school and social events.

But, not on this night—I had a preview, as I was invited to her house to prepare for the dance we were to attend. She wore a garment that was more startling and glamorous than anything any of us had seen on one of our peers. The dress was forest green silk velvet. Fitted at the waist, the hemline fell to about two inches below the knee. The neckline was movie star cut. It was low with a fluted ruffle along the daring edge. It could not have been worn by anyone else. I saw this as a moment of perfect beauty.

I have, in my time, viewed in life and on the stage, many beautiful designs, but this one, appearing as it did, on my friend, at the threshold of our social emergence, was a forecast of the visual maturity that was coming for us all.

The Linen Dresses

They were purchased at Leeds, and Haber and Company, clothing stores on F Street in downtown Washington, DC in the spring of 1964. Linen clothing was fashionable at the time. It was made to be worn for church, afternoon luncheons, teas, or early evening engagements.

I had yet to fully develop a true style of my own. My fashion sense was dictated by two things: what my Grandmother, who called me "The Queen," thought was attractive, and how thin I was. I recall this was the last period before my abdication from my role as "The Queen." This was the prelude into my, if you will, funkier side when I wore mini skirts and easy to shred and shrink paper and wool crepe dresses.

As styles went, the linen dresses were representative of the last bastion of a more formal way of dressing that was disappearing. My Grandmother and I always shopped in volume. On one such trip, I came home with eight of these outfits in big shopping bags.

The first of these was the most impressive. The dress, cut to a tiny size eight sheath, was complemented by a bright yellow colored overcoat/duster and had, mixed into the same yellow: white, hot pink and taupe flowers. It had a cowl neckline and was sleeveless. Once zipped into this dress, it was not possible to draw breath. It was perfect for me.

I recently saw a garment like this one in the same color palette in the display window of a well known store in the Dupont Circle area of Washington, DC. I was stopped in my tracks by the potent memory of this two-piece ensemble.

The second outfit was a sleeveless white linen dress, also in a size eight. This one had a slightly looser fit and was accented with a black organdy voile collar organized in points. The white fabric was a polka dot design, popular at the time. I must admit, that although the dress was a pretty feminine one, the effect was a bit clown-like. I usually felt fat in this dress because of the looser fit.

The third outfit was a two-piece canary yellow suit with a tight skirt and top. The sleeves of the top were lined with a bright orange linen trim. I liked this design because of the slim fit.

The fourth outfit was hot pink with an accent color of Kelly green. This dress, made of a thinner material, sported a back zipper and was somehow not too tight or loose. It was not a very interesting dress.

The fifth outfit was fitted in a bright lime green with black trim. This was the second prettiest garment in the linen collection. It was very tight in the same spirit of outfit number one and was usually accessorized with black patent leather shoes with delicately cut matching flowers on their pointed toes.

The sixth outfit was a combination of linen and gingham in a soft brown and white check. The skirt was in a white linen A-line wrap around style. I never liked it. The attached top had three-quarter length sleeves in the brown and white checkered fabric with flat pearlized buttons. I wore this outfit many times. This was more because it offered a fashion transition, than because I enjoyed it or felt comfortable in it. I wore this with what were probably the simplest, prettiest and most serviceable pair of shoes I ever owned. They were white sling backs in a tiny stamped pebbled leather. With a one-and-a-half-inch block heel that went click-click-click on the pavement as if keeping track of time as I walked down the street . . . "Do wah diddy diddy dum diddy do."

The seventh and eighth outfits were also symbolic of things to come. These were the very first of a procession of what I like to think of as the black cocktail dresses. My entrée to a more adult feeling of evening attire. One of these was a black square-necked dress with long white ruffled sleeves to the wrist in cascading strips of voile. What can I say?

Last but, may I say the following, not least, was the straight-as-an-arrow cocktail dress with the tiny v at the lowered neckline and the one-and-a-half-inch shoulder straps. I still dream I am the girl who can fit into this dress, and these days often wear ill-fitting clothing, while pretending this is true. This always inspires that pursed-lipped look I so look forward to from friends. The dress was a beautiful weighted simple black crepe dress. The cut and the whisper of seductiveness told a story of coming attractions, and *that* is definitely an entirely different book.

Maidenform

Taupe or pink. Those were the colors. I used to have a little pinkish-taupe Maidenform slip. It had a thin elastic waistband, and a ribbon threaded through the trim at the hemline. I used this short slip as a barometer for my figure at all times. It was better than all of my other monitoring garments. I carried it with me for years until it no longer fit and had no elastic left at all.

Sometimes in that wistful mood that so often accompanies looking at second-hand clothing, I search for those old labels and the gentle colors and fabric of my distant youth. I feel they had one thing in common. They were quietly feminine and seemed almost alive to the ones who wore them. That, I believe, had less to do with the garment, and more to do with the times in which they were created.

The audience was different. Undergarments were private articles worn for function and fit. The details beneath clothing were not considered to be street wear. The styles had a loveliness about them, not clandestine, really, but almost holding a woman's personal esteem, draping her attributes with layers of refined detail, a private curtain of beauty between the woman and the world.

The Zebra Room

When I was old enough to drive a car, my father told me to take singing lessons. He insisted that if I did not do this, I would not be permitted to get my driver's license. This is how I began to study singing.

I worked, privately, with the same teacher that I had for voice lessons at Mount Vernon Seminary. Her name was Madame Lida Brodenova. With her as my guide, I learned songs by Claude Debussy, an opera aria by Giacomo Puccini, and numerous songs from the musicals of stage and screen. By the time I was 16, I was ready to do a little concert at school and a private concert at the home of my teacher. My high school debut featured me singing a duet from *Brigadoon*, 'The Heather on the Hill.' Afterwards, my father said, "Go ahead and get the license, but don't worry about the singing, you really are not very good." My second attempt was the private concert about a year later. This was my effort to improve and to change his mind about my talent. I did not succeed this time, either.

This marked the formal beginning of it: the drinking. I was invited after the concert to go with a few friends to the Zebra Room on the corner of McComb and Wisconsin Avenue. We must have looked the part, for we got in with little trouble. We were about 17, but were legally supposed to be 18. The main idea, for me, was that I had failed. This liquid was comforting and uplifting. I continued to try singing and I still do. I drank for another 21 years before I stopped. Somehow one was always linked to the other. In one avenue I lost myself, in the other I was found.

Only now that the drinking is gone do I truly sing. It is not for my mother, my father, or anyone else's approval. I am led to this. My song is no longer my own. It is a flowing river of faith passing into the air, on a long breath, from an old, old soul.

The Pink Mohair Coat

In the '60s, I would often take a long, multidirectional, confusing, absolutely guaranteed to get me totally lost path to the District of Columbia train depot: Union Station. In those days, I drove either a Corvair Monza, or a borrowed Ford Fairlane. I remember the mohair spring coats I wore on some of these drives. I had a pink one and a white one. Both coats were lined in silk. I liked the pink one best. I smoked cigarettes at the time, and I used a silvery metal lighter studded with sapphires. This slid neatly into the side pocket of my mohair coat. It felt as though I carried a pocket coronation crown as I moved through the station rotunda to see my boyfriend off to the military academy.

This young man lived with his family in a windmill on the old Walter Reed Army complex. Comings and goings in those times were easier. There was room to feel the romance of these historic buildings and to participate in their atmosphere.

Much later, around 1966, when I went to Union Station, I found that it seemed to be fading entirely. The experience of buying a ticket was lonesome. There were very few travelers in line. I could proceed directly to the window.

One of the last moments I recall from this period was on an evening in August 1966 when I attended a Beatles concert in the DC Stadium. After the concert we parked outside of Union Station. I went in to use the ladies room, and there was no one in there at all. I walked across the endless marble expanse like a lone streetwalker.

The next time I visited on a trip home from college, the decor was completely gone. It was gone. Gone. In place of the old grandeur was a modern design that hid all traces of architectural grace.

And so it was that a place that had been a touchstone for thousands became a barren wasteland. A palette of scientific white, no longer a witness to the passage of civilization through its doors. In fact, it was seldom visited. It was both shocking and sad to see this place vanishing, in the way of so much of the rest of old Washington DC.

But in the midst of this great disappearance, there arose a public outcry, and a movement began to uncover the lost details, which, as they were restored, slowly revealed the soaring golden windows and statues overlooking the great halls.

The times will never be the same, nor will the sense of old sanctuary, but each time I enter this restored space a piece of me falls back into place and prepares me for what remains of my journey. I am much older now, but still, at heart, the beautiful, hopeful young girl in the pink mohair coat.

The Coral Evening Dress

This was a column of coral crepe. It was purchased in a dress shop in Westwood Village near the Super Giant and The Drug Fair. This was the spring of 1966, and the dress was a size six. It was worn for the commencement dance of our Mount Vernon Seminary graduating class. The party was held on the rooftop of an old club at the edge of Georgetown on M Street.

In those days we wore special undergarments: merry widows, girdles, and hose. On our heads we wore hair pieces and falls. For this occasion, I wore a collection of faux hair piled on top of my head, *à la Holly Golightly*, which I absolutely did not.

The coral evening dress fit me like a second skin and was accessorized with long gloves to the elbow in pearl-grey satin. I wore a pair of long earrings and a corsage of white gardenias, which my date presented to me upon his arrival. My evening shoes were Quality Craft high heels from Baker's shoe store on F Street. They were dyed to match the gown. I was five foot four and a half inches and with the high heels stood at five foot eight. I was ready for my last evening of high school dancing before the long summer leading up to my departure for college. This was the last evening gown to be worn by the young woman I had groomed myself to be.

I kept this dress during my college years in various closets, usually near the taupe test slip. I did not retrieve it from this placement until my junior year. I showed it to my roommates, who looked at me as if to say, "I hope you do not imagine, for a moment, that you are still able to fit into that dress." It was then that I put the dress into a garment bag to later be disposed of or forgotten—or lost—along with that beautiful, hard won, figure. They probably both float with my other memories, like flags caught on some exotic coral reef—somewhere.

The Wrangler Jeans

Every year our family took a trip to the beach. This would usually be to Bethany Beach, Fenwick Island, Ocean City, or Rehoboth Beach, our destinations to the shorelines of Maryland and Delaware.

We would set out in the car with sandwiches and soda in the cooler, if the drive was made during the day. In the evening we would rest our sleepy heads against the seat backs and doze off.

Our family vacations would last for a week, from Friday evening or very early Saturday morning until Sunday of the following week. In the early years we would rent a beach apartment, and in the '60s, when the family got bigger, a house.

I loved the car trips with the verbal games we played to pass the time on the three-hour ride. There was much less traffic so we would travel all throughout the countryside admiring the farmland and occasional billboards, inevitably stopping at a Tastee-Freez for a frozen custard.

I mostly remember the arrivals and our days of sun bathing where we oiled ourselves and used metallic reflectors to intensify our sunburns. The goal was to glow in the evening light.

To me, there was nothing more beautiful or powerful than the ocean. I loved playing and swimming in it, riding the waves, and fighting the undertow. I loved sitting on its ever moving edge digging for sand crabs and walking along its shore collecting shells. All of this ended for me when I saw the movie, Jaws. I never went into the ocean again. But in those early times, arriving at our destination to the scent of the salt air, local trees, and knotty pine beach cottages was magic. It was like visiting a foreign country. Even the food was different. Between the fresh fish we caught on our bay side fishing trips, to the absolutely fabulous seafood at Phillips Crab house, to the spectacular offerings of junk food and candy on the various boardwalks, we felt we had arrived at last in a family wonderland. In the early years, these trips offered us the same respite we experienced at Christmastime. We were able to enjoy the relaxation and fun of the shore with unfettered hearts, and the experience seemed periodically to knit our family back together.

As time moved on and we neared our own exits from the family nest we brought the trouble with us on the road. Then even the baking sun and the ocean beach could not assist us.

Not even fried food helped.

I still remember that last drive home from the beach in the red Ford Fairlane with my father yelling and the car rocking at hideous speeds on the road. I had the feeling that it would be a miracle if we made it home in one piece, or even if we lived through the night. I never travelled to the beach with my family again.

The most significant memory that I carry from that last trip was of a newly acquired pair of Wrangler jeans, which I bought in a little shop on a side street in Ocean City, Maryland. I held onto them for years but, like my family, they never fit me again. To this day, I long for what was then lost to me.

Old Farm — Spring Hill

After Words

After Words

108

After Words

Getting the Mail

It was almost all over. My mother was now living in Gaithersburg, Maryland. I was a regular visitor from the far corners of wherever. Dad was gone. She was living, tucked away, in a nice apartment with her pretty things around her. She would get up every day to work at her desk. I think she was sorting through all of the details of her life, making preparations to provide for her children. She came to visit me as well, during this time, until finding that she was too weak to travel, she no longer made the trip. As to this period of transition, my mother was fortunate to find a solution that allowed her to keep a home. She surrounded herself with the things that had meaning for her and reflected her history. She thought of this as maintaining her dignity and her independence. This was a special time for her. My mother loved Maryland and Washington, DC. She called them home for as long as she could.

There was a small den/bedroom in the back of this apartment. It had two windows and furniture from our old family rooms. I enjoyed sitting and reading in this room, especially in the late spring and summer when the screens were in the windows. Here I read books from my mother's library. I loved the ones by Rosamunde Pilcher and Anne Rivers Siddons, both of whom my mother read avidly. These women write with great soulfulness about family and relationships, and with imagination and sensitivity in matters related to regional customs. I felt a special connection to my mother as I read and discussed with her the books she had chosen for herself.

On these comforting afternoons, as I looked out the window, I could see my mother as she walked to the mailbox by way of the path along the back of the apartment building. In the summer, she would cross the lawn slowly in the humidity she so loved, or, if in the winter, through the snow. For the cooler trips, she would prepare for about 45 minutes, dressing to go on this sojourn. She made these trips independently, and when she could no longer manage it alone, it would be she who would sit in the window to wait for me to retrieve the daily mail. However it arrived, once she had it in her possession, she would go to her desk to pour over the contents. These would include letters, bills, junk mail, random advertisements, greeting cards and sometimes, an invitation.

I would sit quietly in the other room listening to the sounds of my mother sifting through the memories of her life in the District of Columbia, and then in Maryland, her home ports. They were places of bearing and raising of children, of bounty, beauty and some heartbreak. It seemed that what was left she held reverently in her hands.

I now sit at my own desk, realizing, in a similar way, that the past has faded forever. And now I sift through the papers and letters and the particulars of my life, as I piece together, in my own style, something of grace, something I might pass on to others.

Standing By the Sink

This was her command post. My mother stood at the sink all hours of the day and night, running her household as if from the helm of a ship. Here was an anchor, her place of safety.

At the sink, she cried her tears, issued her orders, held on for dear life, said her prayers, washed the lettuce, did the dishes, lost and then found things in the disposal, peeled the potatoes, laughed at jokes, barked directions for children's homework, picked up the pieces, muttered oaths, offered advice, sang hymns and Christmas carols, and stood in silence.

At the sink, she waited for my father to come home safely, listened for the arrivals of visiting family, attended to baking cookies, watched for meals to be ready for the table, and held her breath, anticipating the announcement we would soon be moving again. Here she waited to see what she might have done wrong, organized what needed cleaning, thought about what bills should be paid, and wondered how long my father would stay on the phone with his mother, before coming to see her in the kitchen.

She could execute tasks of any size from this, her touchstone. Through all of the years of my mother's life, some blessed, some tragic, this tiny pool offered her an oasis of peace and the illusion of stability. In an odd way, it seemed the sum of the space she felt was truly her own.

My dear mother is gone now. She worked hard and against many, many unpredictable odds. She married young and had five children before she was 35 years old. It was too much, even in the days when life was easier. Comings and goings had an unhurried charm that is gone today. She performed miracles, this courageous woman. It must have been her faith and a belief that all of us were good people. She was so terribly young for all that she carried bravely on her shoulders.

I can only hope that in some way, in the final years of her life, I brought to her, in my desire to love and participate, some happiness, and that she knew how grateful I was that she was my mother.

Now, as I stand at my own sink holding on for dear life, I consider hers, and continue to remember and honor her heroism, her grace, and her boundless, ever faithful love.

The Evening is Drawing In

One evening in 2016, as I was on my way with a friend to a community Army Corps of Engineers Restoration Advisory Board (RAB) meeting, we drove through Spring Hill. This was the last Washington, DC neighborhood I lived in with my family. Spring Hill was a development of WC&AN Miller, just as my first two homes in Spring Valley had been. The houses in the neighborhood were uniformly built to a large scale. This location was barely over the District/Maryland line but was still considered to be a Washington, DC address.

I recall, on one of my pilgrimages to the old neighborhoods, noticing all the service trucks along the curb of these expansive, well built homes, most of them with writing on the doors that read "pool maintenance." The key here is money, lots and lots of money. Growing up with an illusion of plenty, I did not think of it much. I took for granted, for a while, the level of privilege, wealth, and opportunity I had experienced. When it was gone, I got the picture.

In the '60s, the whole area was landscaped, and the feeling was one of spaciousness and a lightly planted streetscape. Now fifty-some years later, it looked to be more of a woodland palace with mature homes settled under verdant green canopies. My old house was a three storied red brick structure. On the second level, it had white wrought iron balconies that ran across the front of the house. Now, as I recall, the overall effect was elegant, impressive, and expensive as hell. This beautiful dwelling was not my favorite. Two things I remember being fond of were the giant backyard with the tall trees, and my elegant bedroom with its outdoor balcony and private bathroom.

My father purchased this house by candlelight on a whim. In so doing, he stretched himself and his mother, my Grandmother, way beyond their collective means. The financial gong had sounded years before, but this new expenditure paid no heed to its warning and would eat away at the family reserve of principle and principal.

This was the house where I perfected my ability to unpack entire households of goods and clothing. In so doing, I would set the current stage in my unfolding family drama.

This was also the house where I forged my relationship with trying on clothing to monitor, and maintain a newly achieved slenderness. The goal was to remain as thin as everyone wanted me to be. The greatest fear I had was to hear someone say, "It looks like you have put on weight," or, my favorite, "I think you have gained about five pounds."

This evening, as I rode by with my friend, I saw the old pale pink brick house standing under the full trees. Now, the house was trimmed in black with a shiny front door, shutters and the wrought iron balconies of the second floor.

All the elements were luxuriously dark and elegant, with gold hardware accents and warm lights glowing through the full trees. The impression was of an old gold Queen replete with a theatrical history, a dark beauty resplendent in crown jewels waiting for night to fall.

And I thought, time is running out. This is no longer the street of my mid-teen years. This is someone else's time and turn in this house. It is they who now stand in the shadows of the coming evening in their yard.

"And you," I thought to myself, "are still carrying the memory of your life in this place. So, it must be time to release this story—time to let go, and share all its beauty, truth and horror."

In that moment, with the visual elegance, the allure of the house, and the specter of that Queen, it seemed as if I were seeing instead, a Victorian funeral cortege. All these years later, I realized I was still deep in mourning for my unresolved past, and I knew it was time to shed the dark garments and lift the veils of grief.

I felt willing to tell the tale of my heart. And the sight of this place at deep dusk brought it all back—all of it—as a gift.

Do You Believe in Magic?

Yes, I believe, I do. I suppose I could call it coincidence, but no, I think magic might be the better word, or perhaps, destiny. In my parents' life together, every birthday or anniversary fell in the 20s of the month. This applied to their own birthdays, their wedding anniversary, and to their five children's birthdays.

The last house in which my parents resided was on a street named Bradley Boulevard. This was in Bethesda, Maryland. When my father passed away, my mother sold the home. After a time living with my sister, and then in her own apartment in Gaithersburg, Maryland, she moved to her last address on York Street, in New Haven, Connecticut, where she lived in an apartment next to my brother and his wife near the Yale campus. Here she had her own little haven, all her belongings surrounding her, quiet independence with family right next door. She enjoyed seeing the youth about her, coming and going, following their educational paths. Alongside of those who were beginning their professional lives, she was content with memories of her own life.

It was a solution she had for her Bethesda dream, to live in an urban apartment at the end of her life, where she could enjoy having family come to visit, going to restaurants, venturing out on little shopping trips and getting her hair done. She ended her days here.

Upon their deaths, both of my parents were cremated. Their final resting place is at Arlington National Cemetery. They now are in the beautiful columbarium on these hallowed grounds. They are remarkably placed between two streets: Bradley and York.

So yes, I do believe. I believe in magic.

Dear Mom and Dad:

I am at the cemetery today. I came to see you. I miss you and I am now at work writing some of our story. I am so grateful for the love you both gave to me. You passed on to your great strength and will to survive, as well as weight of your deep sadness and struggle. I shared all aspects and none of us were to blame for the circumstances we faced as a family. I only wish you could have lived longer to enjoy the former and be loosened from the paralyzing grip of the latter.

Father, your life was too short for what you might have shared and received from the world. It is with you in mind, and with love, that I now pull these threads of memory from your broken heart into my own, now strung like a harp. Strings, not of discord, but reminiscent of the many blessings you wished for yourself and for loved ones. None of it was your fault. I love you, Father, with all of my heart.

Mother, I miss you every day. As my world revolves, I think of you and your everlasting courage to live. When the carpet of my memory rolls forward, in red, with this history, I promise to, step by step, reflect your beauty. Not by hiding the truth, but by illuminating the whole picture, with all of its sharp contrasts. I am remembering the miracle of our survival, and the love we shared at the end.

Love, Martha

Written at the intersection of Bradley and York—
John Barry Letterman, AM3USN, 1924-1988
Doris Benson Letterman, 1926-2008.

After Words

The Tourist Home

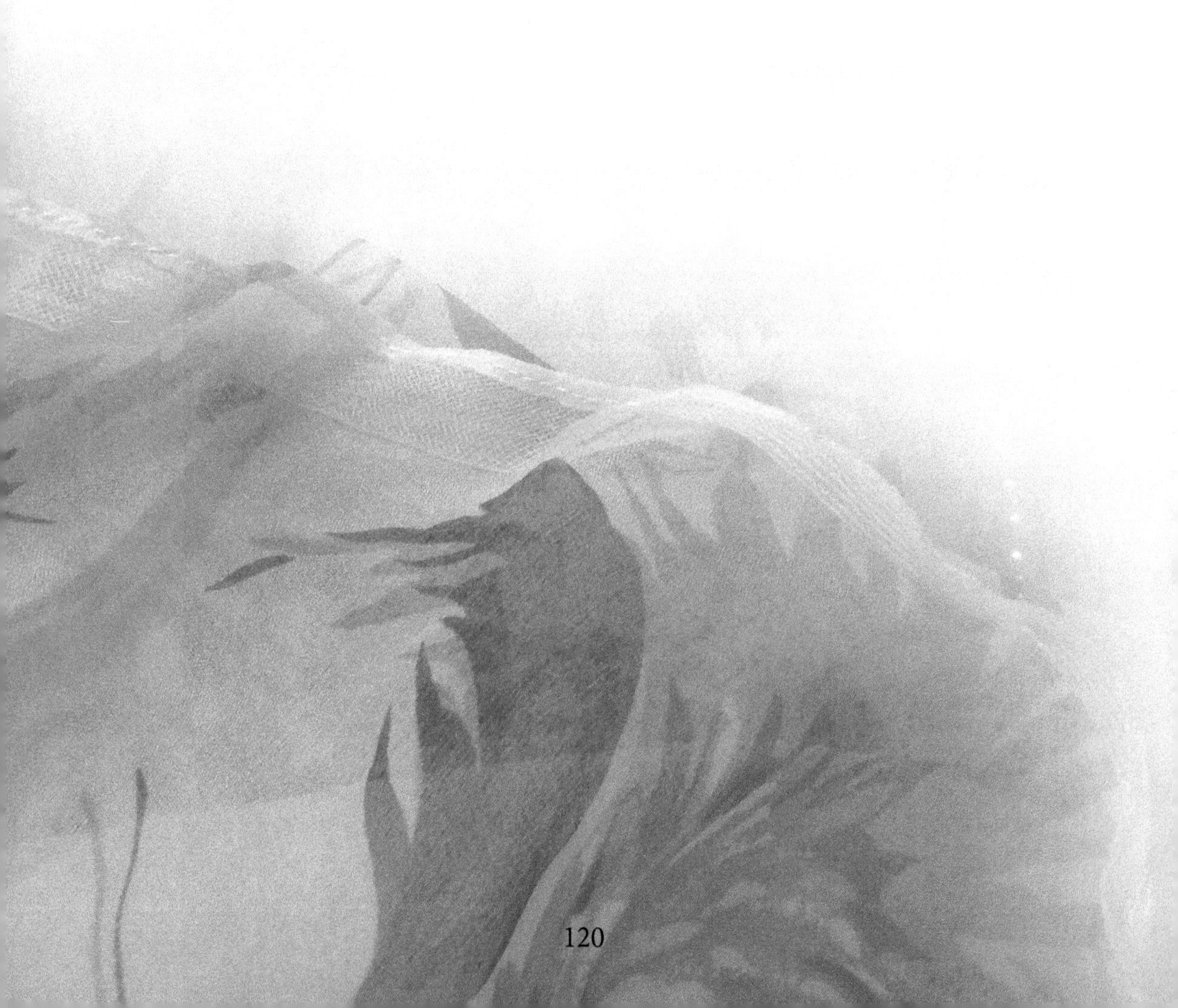

The Tourist Home

Buried Treasure

Last night I dreamt I was in the alley behind the fallen Tourist Home. I was searching through the rubble under the skirts of the old southern porches, whose tattered remnants hung like threadbare petticoats. Here, I looked for the remains of my old presence in the world, for this is surely where I left it behind.

Along with the joy of having found a tiny spot in the world that will serve as I wind the clock for my last hours, is an unspeakable sadness. As the evening draws to a close, I realize it is time for a new story. It is one of gratitude and acceptance for a life lived fully. I realize the time has come for others to take their turns. I just sometimes wish they could see me too. It is poignant, to be at a point in life when one becomes socially invisible.

Coming awake, I wonder how it is that I can ask to be acknowledged, when I can barely find myself. But in this, at least I know my task is to keep digging, to make my pile, and to hold each piece of my history, item by item, up to the light, and to say, after all, that I am someone too, and I am content.

Watching It Come Down

One minute I was moving through the now emptied hallways of my family's life of privilege. The next thing I knew, I was across the street in an upholstered rocker with mahogany handles, staring out at the demolition. That was all that was left of the Tourist Home after the crane with the ball and chain crashed into it, leveling it to the ground while I watched.

At the time, I could not comprehend what was happening. I must have been in a state of shock. I cannot even begin to fathom what my grandparents must have felt, to see their life's work and history fall into piles at their feet. Now, from where I sit, I can feel it all, as they must have felt it then, while brick by beautiful brick their home tumbled to the street below. Panes of glass, chandeliers, pocket doors, transoms, miles of tile, marble and enamel, plaster walls, window and door frames, mantle pieces and heavy crowning mirrors, linoleum, railings—hundreds of architectural details—memories reduced to dust.

I suppose there might have been a moment or two when we looked to the partnership, which built the new Letterman House, with hopefulness. That dream was soon to fall from our hands, but at the time, the illusion of a path forward for the family business was a comfort.

I still cannot bear any of this, and it is more than 50 years later. It is not very brave, I realize, to be paralyzed by a loss that occurred so long ago. I can forgive myself for this. It was during this period we moved from our beloved childhood neighborhood, Spring Valley. Atlantic City, my home away from home, was in disrepair. The Tourist Home had been demolished, and old Washington, DC had begun to vanish. All at once, everything that was my home was gone, or disappearing.

I understand this is the burden of grief and regret I have carried all of my life. I now accept this and can let the history go. This is the house I have sought for the past 30 years. I can now rebuild this house, if only with paper, and not to live in, for when one has had such a place in life, in such a time, there is no replacement.

Therefore, I have come to my lifestyle as a pilgrim, or a gypsy. I understand the desire to live in 100 rooms. This is my journey of gratitude, a blessing in the corridors of my time on earth.

What I can do, as an older woman, and an actress, is stand in the scarlet cinders of my past and recall it theatrically. I can do this in remembrance and gratitude for the amazing individuals who crafted it and then shared it with me. I can say to the world, or to anyone who will listen, that once upon a time, at 21st and F Streets, there stood a small city of rooms where travelers, family, and friends came to live. And that as their lives played out in its joyful resonant halls, for a minute, a day, a week, or for years at a time, a full-length technicolor moving picture was made.

My Grandmother Letterman's Closet

The story of the Tourist Home began with my Grandmother Letterman's buying one victorian townhouse in the 2100 block of F Street in the Foggy Bottom neighborhood of Washington, DC. Over the years my grandparents were able to purchase neighboring properties until there were ten of these buildings, connected to one another. From beginning to end of my grandparents' tenure in this establishment, they chose—from all of the one hundred rooms—one. In this one room there beat the heart of the Tourist Home. It was a single rectangular chamber, and had no closet space whatsoever.

Therefore, my Grandmother Letterman did not have a typical closet. Dresses, suits, blouses, coats and furs were hung on the back of a door in her bedroom at the Tourist Home.

On the right hand side of her bed she had a night stand designed on the outside to look like it had three drawers. There were even three metal drawer pulls, but only one, big drawer.

This is where she kept many of her pairs of shoes. My favorite, within the jumbled collection, was a pair of soft red shoe boots. They had very pointed toes and small heels. The boots were fashioned to fit snugly by lacing up the front to the ankle. Among the rest of the shoes were serviceable spectator pumps, as well as patent and soft leather shoes with "sensible" heels appropriate for ascending and descending the hundreds of steps that needed to be navigated in her "home." Also tossed, in the midst of the prettier shoes, was a pair of see-through grey galoshes, which were very practical during the winter's slush and spring rains of DC.

My Grandfather's police uniforms, suits, coats, and shirts hung from the door at the foot of his bed on the left side of the room. This was also the door that had the Coke machine on the other side of it in the hall. Hats, men's in one stack, women's in another, were piled in the corners from the floor to the ceiling in big boxes. The boxes were round and square, designed and plain, and made of sturdy "good looking" cardboard. Smaller items were stuffed into the drawers of his tall dresser and into her double-sided, six drawer, taupe-colored French Provincial bureau. This was straight across the room on the wall opposite the entrance, and her clothes on the back of the door were reflected in the mirror of her double-sided, six drawer, taupe-colored French Provincial bureau.

Items always tumbled from my grandmother's dresser, which was crammed with lingerie: slips, "drawers" or step-ins, corsets, girdles, socks, and stockings all together. This was a mixture as eccentric as my Grandmother herself. Remarkably, she did not have much in the way of clothing. She had suits and day dresses, of course, and sun dresses in the spring. But, as the years went on, she preferred the comfort of homemade garments, dresses with velvet-trimmed, capped sleeves, which she would top off with a shawl-collared, ranch mink coat and a hat to match. She was more for the accessories. She loved to wear pins, big charm bracelets, and all kinds of wonderful rhinestone costume jewelry, and, of course, her diamond rings.

And then there was the perfume. This was not always the expensive variety she choose for my mother, and eventually for all of the aunts, cousins and granddaughters. These scents were really not too subtle. Tabu, Chantilly, Emeraude, Tweed, Tigress, Woodhue and always the exceptions of Chanel N°5 and Arpège by Lanvin.

The items on the dresser top were equally varied. There were jars of cold cream, boxes of face powder and compacts with jeweled tops. There were tiny containers of rouge, pill boxes, and various elegant presentations of old and new recipe lipstick. There were tubes of Bengay, tins of Cuticura, jars of Vaseline, bottles of liniment, and Vicks VapoRub in a vaporizer. It was all haphazard and bohemian, with round, gold filigree dresser trays, loose powder and powder puffs and linen runners strewn about. There was Tussy Deodorant in a jar wrapped in swirled aluminum, perfume bottles of all sizes, tins of tooth powder, and false teeth in a glass half-filled with a mixture of water and Polident. Green mini Coca-Cola bottles, half full, full, warm, or chilled were always a feature.

And then there was the money. It was all over the place. There were copper pennies, stacks and rolls of buffalo nickels, quarters, fifty-cent pieces, silver dollars, one dollar bills and even two dollar bills. Jewelry boxes were full to overflowing with costume jewelry. Crystal, rhinestones in all colors, pearl necklaces, bracelets with semiprecious stones and beads. There was a vast collection of colorful pins. There were scarves and silk flowers with silvery pins, greeting cards and keys.

Along the right side of the room was a curved wall with two large windows covered with drapes and venetian blinds. There was a radiator across this part of the room. The safe was to the left in its own separate alcove. Prominently situated on the top of the covered radiator were the papers and adding machines. There were ledgers, legal pads, and mid-sized steno pads filled with notes concerning the running of the business. There was a green velvet rocking chair in the corner that my Grandmother loved to sit in as she considered the details of her life. There, she would laugh and talk and make plans for all that she wanted to do for her family.

None of these elements alone cast the spell. It was all of it, all of the time, in its unrelenting consistency, that held me in its thrall.

I stayed with my grandparents in that room for years on end. I knew it like a second skin. Sometimes, I would relax there in the winter, listening to the clanging of the radiators, or in the summer, to the simple lullabies of the whir of an electric fan, or the DC buses going by, and I knew that nothing in my life would ever offer such a universe. That is certainly not to say the rest was not without its own character, comfort, and value. But this was the heart of it for me. As I lay there, with the sounds of my snoring Grandfather, and my Grandmother talking, talking, talking, I would drift, unwilling, off to sleep. I felt as though there could never ever be enough time for this love.

Sunday Dinners

Every week after church my family drove downtown to the Tourist Home for Sunday dinner. We arrived around noontime and stayed until about 5 o'clock in the afternoon. After our meal—after eating— we visited. Then we would take an afternoon nap. This was followed by more visiting, conversation, and, finally, our good-byes. Over the years, we had two dining suites. The first was in 2032 and then in the house all the way at the end of our real estate at 2026. Once the dining room and kitchens were moved to this location, they stayed until the end.

In this last dining room was a large mahogany table and chairs that seated about twelve people comfortably. There was a matching corner cabinet and a large scale secretary/breakfront to compete the lovely ensemble. As incidentals in the room, but no less important to us, were a small telephone table with an attached chair and two small sideboards at either end of the room. The dining table was beautifully set with linens, china, and crystal. There were two silver candelabras on the table with a matching tea and coffee service on a tray. The china was a delicate white Lenox and had the gold trim that was often its signature.

A typical meal would be fried chicken, mashed potatoes and creamed gravy, green beans cooked in smoked bacon, succotash, coleslaw, freshly baked biscuits, olives, pickles and relishes, with peach pie and vanilla ice cream for dessert.

We would all sit around the table eating, laughing and talking. When we were finished, we would practically pass out, we were all so full. Later in the afternoon, we would have hot tea and cookies at the table before getting ready to go home. These were wonderful, sharing times for my family. What I remember the most, apart from the delicious, delicious food was the sense of closeness these events provided. There was a special bond formed over those meals and conversations that was unforgettable and really provided us with an oasis of peace and connection. We were happy there.

Cockroach

No wonder we used a chamber pot!!!!

There were 100 rooms in the Tourist Home in Foggy Bottom in Washington, DC. When I visited as a child for a weekend, or for longer periods in the summer, I would stay with my grandparents in their room. When I got older, I was allowed to choose from any of the unoccupied units for my visits and became even better acquainted with the details and decor of the unusual guest rooms.

But, when I was young, I stayed in their room on a roll-away bed between their twin beds under the canopy of clothes that hung on the back of the entrance door. I probably favor sleeping on cots and small beds to this day because I am reminded of the little ones I would sleep on at the Tourist Home, and sometimes during the summer in Atlantic City. So there I would be on the roll-away, with my Grandmother to my right, and my Grandfather to my left. It was a tight squeeze. From this position, however, I could see our summer luggage peeking out from below my grandparents' beds.

Sometimes during the night, in answering nature's call, I would get up and need to visit "the toilet"—as my Grandmother called it—I can still hear her say, "Martha Ann, do you need to go to the toilet?"

We had a chamber pot, but I could not bring myself to use it—well—not at first, anyway.

But after a while . . .   You see, it was like this:

The family bathroom was located six lobbies away. To reach it, you needed to travel a network of hallways to 2026 where the living room, dining room, and family bathroom were located. Also in residence, in this distant spot, was the house mouse, oddly, named John, also my Father's name. This creature, as I distinctly recall, was not in the least bit particular about whose path he crossed on his nocturnal forays across the landscape in the Tourist Home.

Now, let's not forget, this is the South. Of an evening, about 200 three-quarter to one-inch long cockroaches would skitter across the surface of the hallway, kitchen and bath areas when I turned on the lights. I would arrive barefooted making a final approach to the dark mint green bathroom with the film of cooking on the walls. This pilgrimage lent worlds of new meaning to "Snap, Crackle and Pop." These rooms were not dirty, just lived in, and the buildings were very, very old. It came with the territory. In the end, after what felt like a small creature war, I would journey the distance back to my shared room.

As I made this trek, I had time to consider my alternative to the matter at hand. In this moment, the pink enamel chamber pot with the black trim and the little handle on the side beckoned like a "First Family of Virginia" heirloom. And I could hear my Grandmother exclaim, "Why yes, indeedy, Martha Ann, that is FFV."

Bernard

Well . . .

Bernard was an older African American gentleman who did everything around the place, and he was, what we might have called today, our handyman. My Grandmother loved Bernard. He and Mary—I am not sure if they were related—would arrive daily to maintain and care for the complicated machine that was the Tourist Home.

My primary image of Bernard was of him maneuvering the old Hoover vacuum cleaner. I always loved the comforting sound of it. Somehow it held, in its unique music, the promise of a new day.

There were nine lobbies in the buildings, each needing Bernard's attention. Sometimes in the afternoon, I would find Bernard lying on the floor in one of our 100 rooms, passed out, a bottle of liquor in a brown paper bag in his hand, the vacuum cleaner still serenading, its visor-like lamp in the front blazing at his face, focusing like a row of foot-lamps in a vaudeville hall, to feature his spectacular alcoholism.

We all felt so sorry for old, bone-weary, paper-thin, rickety, rackety, lazy, tragic Bernard.

But, I think Bernard felt sorry for all of us. He certainly cared for us and for the house. He made it all work. We all played our parts. As he showed up for his performance, he would cast his showstopping rheumy eyes upon us. If we had looked back at him, we would have known, instantly, that he saw what awaited us.

I can tell you what was waiting for me. It was around the corner from where I stood, three blocks away, in a church fellowship hall. This was the place where people like Bernard and later myself could gather to exchange help and support. In those days there was not as much information as there is now for these venues of assistance. Also . . . one has to be ready.

So, men like Bernard rode themselves like horses, taking the work, community and kindness where they found it, often spending all their hard-earned wages on alcohol. I remember Bernard, long, tall, skinny in his hat, as we toiled along, side by side, in those hot summers at the Tourist Home. I know we could not have saved him, but I do wonder if he did not, in his own way, save us.

Cooking with Grease

Everything I ate at the Tourist Home—well almost everything—was cooked in grease. Crisco, bacon fat, chicken fat, and lard were some of the chief ingredients, and I loved them!!

Pie crusts for peach, apple, cherry, rhubarb, mincemeat and pumpkin were drizzled with it and were among my favorite desserts. Breakfast pancakes, eggs, sausage, bacon and hominy grits were suitably saturated. What's for dinner? Pork and lamb chops, hot dogs, chicken, tomatoes, potatoes and greens. Really, any food was fair game for frying.

The pans we used for this cooking were large cast iron affairs. My Aunt Betty, my Grandmother and my Grandfather Letterman would often grab the handles of those "great big" cast iron skillets from the lit burners of the gas stove. The cotton or linen towels they used to pick them up would often catch fire. My dear and eccentric relatives would then arrive at the table in flames. These exciting events usually took place in the kitchen, while the dining room experience was slightly more civilized.

The hot, heavy meals were routinely enjoyed in sweltering kitchens and humid dining rooms with nothing to ward off the oppressive heat but old, rattling, dusty window or table fans. In the chilly District winters, the still warm serving rooms would be so cozy and full of aroma, the atmosphere would envelop me like a cloak.

Yet, as fun and delicious as those meals were, they were fool's bargains—and would later cause me to willingly submit to the lure of heavy, fattening, sugary foods.

In the end, the price was high indeed. My Grandmother died of colon cancer, and my Grandfather, my Aunt, and my father all passed away from diet-related heart disease and failure.

I arrived at these tables, riding high on the hog. I rode out with no regrets, blissfully unaware of the downside. And, I was, until recently, unable to find my way up and out from either the grips of any of these memories, or from the FOOD.

The Department Stores

These were not stores. They were cities. From the smallest to the largest, they were theatres for whole societies of professionals who stood ready to serve their audiences. Built like layer cakes, they catered to every aspect of life. From the tiniest whim, to the greatest desires, and to practical everyday needs, they served their many tiers of merchandise and style. These stores were a home away from home for me.

Just as the old railroad depots and hotels had been temples for transportation and hospitality, so it was now with the retail venues. The ones my Grandmother and I frequented were located in downtown Washington, DC on F Street in the 1940s and 1950s, and for a short while in the 1960s: Julius Garfinckel's, Jelliffs, Hecht's, Woodward and Lothrop, and Kann's.

My favorites were "Garfinckel's," at the top of F, and "Woodies," at the intersection of 11th and F. We thought of these stores as palaces, main events on our promenade. The long blocks between them were full of other marvelous venues for hats, shoes, candy, jewels, and clothing. Of course, Reeves Tea Room and the Old Ebbitt Grill were there to satisfy any palate looking for good food and old world atmosphere. The side streets held magic as well, in the inviting rooms of The Latch String, Galt's jewelers, and Rosendorf Evans Furs.

All of my rites of passage were recognized with gifts from these stores. Early school dresses and shoes, confirmation gowns, first perfumes, first evening gowns and faux fur jackets, first silk stockings, first seasonal decorations, first engraved special occasion cards, first Easter bonnets and outfits. Over the years, this was virtually a parade of beautiful, beautiful items and collections.

For all occasions, and in all manner of moods, on our shopping excursions, we sang our refrain "Let's go to F Street!" There was never a sense of uncertainty—this was the diversion we sought. We just grabbed our little handbags and our store charge cards, and full of any feeling that had us in its grip, flung our arms into the air to hail a Yellow or a Diamond cab to take us home to the thriving glory of old downtown Washington, DC on F.

But . . .

Most special of all was when the holidays came and downtown became a feast for the eyes and the heart. Decorations went up in the stores after Thanksgiving and their windows overnight became theatres. It was customary to get dressed up to travel to the beautiful displays to see the magic stories that were so often presented in the glass showcases. It seemed that the weather always cooperated and so we had snowflakes to go with the retail presentations. The worlds of make believe and the fantastic beauty of the decor were lavish, detailed and so imaginative. The experience I had as a child that I shared with my family during this season of birth and joy were defining aspects of life. If today I am often unusually blue during a time when so many seem to be in possession of great spirit, it is because I miss these days, these customs and these memories of family. And I miss the vintage beauty in decor and personal costume. I am happy to live with gratitude in the present but I am truly aware of the very different special style that I was privileged to be raised with. In these busy confusing times today, when I can quiet my mind to be aware of the details around me, I remember that the lifetime of experience has been a great gift, and that in memory I can bring the incomparable beauty of my past to the more spare days of the present and in the mixture find a happy medium to sustain me.

The Latch String

Cafeteria dining at The Latch String in downtown Washington, DC in the 1950s captured the old world charm of the city we loved. The sense of occasion that accompanied a lunch or a dinner at this establishment was palpable.

The old building that housed it was tall and narrow with exterior walls of yellow-white stucco and brown wooden trim. There was an entry door leading into a vestibule serving as a buffer to the elements. The second door of heavy, dark wood was about ten feet further inside.

The main hall was a room of soaring heights, tiled floors, brown wooden ceiling fans, rustic lantern chandeliers, and dark, grooved, paneled side walls with brass hooks for the customers' coats. What coats they were! They were wools and furs and cashmeres and all with matching hats and, for the women, matching handbags. The men carried smart portfolios and briefcases.

I recall especially the outings in late fall and early winter. I stood with my grandparents in long lines, waiting to pass through screens that separated the first floor dining hall from the serving area and the kitchens beyond. Going through what seemed to be gates, I entered a world with selections of food I have never had any to compare with since.

Well . . . almost.

The menu items were listed on a board with white moveable letters. My favorite selections were the creamed chicken on biscuits and the gingerbread with warm lemon sauce. The chicken and biscuit dish was hot, rich, and had about 6,000 calories per serving. The gingerbread was of a texture that was so soft, you really could have used it for a pillow. No one wanted to share this dessert. It was served warm with a lemon sauce that was thick and light simultaneously: it was a perfection of delicacy and tang.

Once we made our choices, we would slide our trays along heated aluminum tracks to the cashier where my Grandmother would pay for our meals. Then we were off to the upstairs dining salons. These we would reach by going up a staircase, that, although wide, was three or four hundred steps up. Well . . . maybe a hundred or two. All the way to the top we would balance our wobbly trays of food. When, by some miracle, we reached the top, we were greeted by a sea of dark wood tables bathed in lantern light, if for the night seating or, in a wash of sunlight streaming through the mullioned windows, if for the afternoon seating.

There was always someone graciously bringing iced water to the table as we took our selections from the trays and put them before us. These meals were underscored by waves of laughter and lively conversations that rippled through the large rooms like music.

In addition to the delectable fare, the mystique of those who dined was undeniable. This was 1950s downtown Washington, DC: political, stylish, sexy, dressy, smart, fragrant, glamorous and alluring. At the end of a meal of an astonishing satisfaction, my Grandmother would take out her pocketbook, open the snap, and remove her make-up bag. From this she would retrieve a two-inch gold tube, take off the cap, and with a tiny nickel side lever, raise up her dark red matte lipstick (usually the variety made with oil, beeswax and bug parts) and apply the vibrant color using the mirror in her jeweled compact for precise detailing.

In the 1960s when we were on our last trips to this hallowed community gathering spot, she would repeat the ritual. Older now, I would be there in my Pink Suit, and my Grandmother would be in one of her home-made dresses topped with a fur coat. On one of our last trips to this spot, she wore an outrageous, hot pink straw hat topped by a veritable garden of flowers. This hat, as I recall, was most embarrassing. I would watch her through narrow, lowered eyelids, gritting my teeth, wanting nothing more than to go shopping. I was now an attractive, nouveau-thin teenager, with an attitude.

What I did not realize then, that I do know now, is that these were moments of exquisite experiential poetry, most of which were about to disappear.

Now, when she performed her traditional beautification ritual, she would not use a mirror, nor would she apply the lip color in the traditional way. She, instead, would open her mouth and put the entire tube in, rolling it around in a circle to create the desired effect. During this period she wore Revlon's Love That Red. I can only think, now that the Latch String is gone, how apt it all was, the action and the color. For nothing short of a wide swipe of scarlet, completely covering a neutral surface, could duplicate, or even hint at the experience of that place, the food it featured, or the society to which it catered.

Soon after, The Latch String, like so many other buildings in DC in the '70s, simply vanished, drawing in its wake a time of less complicated human experience. Now, where it stood, is a giant building of stone and glass. Sometimes when I am in Washington, I walk downtown to the spot directly across the street from the wonderful old place to, speechlessly, stare at the section of the block where, years back, the fire-lit lanterns of The Latch String lured its visitors to enter its environment of irreplaceable character and service.

The Fan

The old black metal table fan with its four silver blades cooled us down in the evenings in my grandparents' room at the Tourist Home. This modest-sized fan, about twelve to fourteen inches tall, made a wonderful soothing sound I have always associated with the feeling that all is well. That particular sound, in the '50s and '60s in Washington, DC in Foggy Bottom, was accompanied by the sound of the small clocks in the room ticking, and the city buses going by our two rectangular side windows.

On the other side of the bedroom wall was the rattle, early on, of Coca-Cola bottles being pulled from the cooler and tops coming off and dropping to the bottom of the receptacle used to collect them. Later, a similar set of sounds came from the bottles as they were pulled from the side of a newer model Coke machine. So we had our ticking clocks, the whirring fan, the city sounds, and the clatter of the bottle tops mixed with the steady clinking of the bottles themselves.

In the winter, we still used the black metal fan, more for its music than for the cooling air. Now, in the season of wind and snow, we had an addition to our little orchestra. It was brought to us by the clanging of steam in the radiators and the high pitched hissing as it warmed our room.

Sometimes in the night, in the distance, we would hear the sound of the desk bell—ding ding—telling us someone needed service. This would add an ornament to our sound. But, mostly, it was the old standbys that carried us into our islands of peaceful slumber.

Tick Tock, Tick Tock

Tick tock, tick tock, tick tock! Big Ben and Baby Ben sat on my grandparents' dressers and on the radiator top—different locations for different years. Only the steady sound of the ticking remained the same. That, and the jarring, but familiar, sound of the alarm in the early wake up hours.

These stand alone clocks, Big Ben and Baby Ben, with their slight, and more robust, tick tocks measured peaceful moments for me as I lay in this room in mists of Vicks VapoRub and a bite in the air stung by the odor of liniment and Bengay ointment.

It seemed the regular ticking of time was measuring a meditation for me long before I knew what that was. A metronome for a little life's music. These small appliances provided a strong, serene presence. Minutes teemed with an enviable normalcy, holding me wide awake to this promise with every tick tock, tick tock of the clock.

Number 4

No wonder I love hotels! No wonder I favor living in tiny spaces with thousands of items of nostalgia and beauty around me. Number 4 was such a place.

Number 4 was on the second floor of the main house of the Tourist Home at 2030 F Street. It was the room next to the room at the top of the stairs. The first on the left in the railroad hallway, this was my Aunt Betty's room. Betty was larger than life. She filled her room with her form and her spirit.

In Number 4 there was a mahogany double bed next to the one window in the room. Across from this was a large wardrobe that held most of her clothes and personal treasures. On top of the wardrobe, piled to the ceiling, were her hat boxes. She, like my Grandmother, her sister Georgie, loved great big hats with flowers covering the crown. A closet to the left side of the armoire held winter coats, additional clothes, rainwear, furs, and shoes.

Betty did have a private bathroom: a tiny, windowless bathroom with a tub, shower, sink and medicine chest. White enamel with black tile trim lined the walls, and the floors were black and white, a mosaic of smaller tiles in marble—all brought together with art deco details and fixtures.

Aunt Betty liked pretty things, but was, in the main, practical in her approach to living and collecting. She worked the front desk and assisted with the demands of running the Tourist Home. She spearheaded the kitchen activity and did a great deal of the cooking. Incredible!!!!!! Not to be missed was Aunt Betty's coleslaw made with mustard, vinegar, a drop of worchestershire, sugar, salt, cabbage, celery and mayonnaise! A bright yellow wow!

Scattered throughout Aunt Betty's room were books, newspapers, magazines, and a vast array of foot care products. All of my family's rooms in this place had the same scent. It was a fabulous mixture of perfume, food, cigar smoke and over-the-counter ailment remedies.

It wasn't any item or event in particular that drew me to my Aunt's room. It was her friendship, her understanding, her memories, her view of the world, her clear-sightedness and her empathy. In the middle of this treasured world she was a dose of reality. She understood the price the family was paying—and would continue to pay—if it did not heed the warning signs and acknowledge the debts that could eventually be called in.

Maybe she was my first brush with hope. Surely, it was a first taste of healing . . . I had already learned to live in my own world as a separate vessel charting a course for survival. In the wheelhouse of Number 4, Betty steadily encouraged me to manage these waters, never once underestimating the shift in the prevailing winds in my family life. She simply offered a forecast of the coming storm.

And so it was, that in Number 4, I built a little sailing vessel to the accompaniment of the news, the radio and television shows of the period and the compassion of my loving Aunt Betty.

My Father's Room

There was a room high up top on 2030 F on the fourth floor, if you counted the basement. The room was situated halfway down the corridor on the right hand side. It was a tiny room with a tiled bathroom tucked in the back left hand corner, with a shower, a sink, and a small window looking out towards the old Red Cross Building. There was a narrow window in the main room with a fire escape just outside. Next to the window was a double bed, a night stand, and a straight-backed chair. There was a lamp on the stand and a floor lamp on the opposite side in the corner next to a gentleman's dresser. Small throw rugs were scattered in the areas left bare of furniture.

During the summers I worked at the Tourist Home. This was the time period when I instituted an almost militaristic approach to making a bed properly, a perfection of turned down edges and tucked in corners.

I went up to this particular room one season when I was routinely performing the duties of my summer job. I looked around at the tiny room and for all my pudginess at the time, felt inexplicably small.

Later that same day, at the completion of my tasks, I told my Aunt Betty about the room I had discovered. She looked at me with the slightest of fading smiles and said, "Well, Martha Ann, that room belonged to your father. That was Big John's little room."

Right then and there, another piece of the puzzle that was my father fell quietly into place.

Reading on the Stoop

I thought it would never end. Entering or exiting the houses, I imagined I would always find spots for my reading. It might be a special chair in one of the many parlors, or outside in an old wrought iron one, under a big fringed canvas umbrella with a floral underside, or on a step of one of the nine stoops.

This was my place, and I moved about as if I owned it. There was no thought to who bought it, who maintained it, what its future would be. No thought, for the moment, to chores or what I might do to be of service. I just took what it gave to me and luxuriated in its various comforts. Wherever I found myself, the Tourist Home set a stage upon which I could read and receive various histories or fictions. I could transport myself within the books with more emphasis than normal—so heightened was my sensitivity to place.

Emerson 2-4795/Sterling 3-5784

Telephones! Everything about them was captivating, from the first accessorizing table and chair tucked into my childhood dining room's corner, with the big fat DC phone book on its shelf and the Ma Bell telephone on the table, to the elegant numbers like our first one: Emerson 2-4795.

It was the same with the prefixes at the Tourist Home: Sterling and District. These seemed particularly apt with all of the unusual out-of-town visitors and the ebb and flow of diplomatic and military guests. It was not just the numbers and the formal prefixes, but the telephones themselves, especially the black downtown models. There was a weight to them. It seemed these creature-like entities provided a lifeline.

I remember these heavy phones in my hands, or resting on my shoulder, as I stowed away in the corners of our hallways and rooms, or sat at the numerous lobby tables in our Tourist Home talking on the phone. I am reminded that I bloomed like a flower in the simple exchange of a word, a greeting, or later a fuller—almost urgent — conversation.

It was as if every talk was a verbal vignette worthy of savoring in the moment, and afterwards as a souvenir. The telephone was how I connected to the world and my friends. It offered me a chance to create something that felt intimate and valuable with words over the wires.

The Evening Constitutions

Everyone has their rituals and their special paths. My Grandfather Letterman was no exception. He had his beat that he walked in Foggy Bottom as a police officer, he had his visits to Hains Point to meet with his maritime comrades, and he had what he called his "Evening Constitutions." I thought he named them thus, because we were close to Constitution Avenue.* That, of course, was not it. It was at that time of day, in the early evening, when he would walk to get his exercise, and sometimes, when I think of it now, to go to some of the local watering holes, like Little Vienna, for a drink with his friends. Mostly, this was his special time away from the worries and demands of the Tourist Home.

Sometimes, when I was visiting, I would be invited to come along for one of these long city walks. The regime of this appealed to me, and the flavor of the city in these days was relaxed and lent itself to longer rambles along its sidewalks and down its lovely boulevards. There were benches to sit on in spacious parks, the great federal buildings to admire, and the monuments glowing in the twilight to inspire.

This was our city, and there was a sense of pride of place that we felt as we made our way through the streets. This walking meditation became a tradition for me and my Grandfather Letterman.

* only to learn later in life the traditional
  terminology: "constitutionals"

Making Lace Blind

At the core of the Tourist Home there was a galvanizing energy which I understand now. It was artistry and vision. My Grandmother Letterman was its chief architect. She passed on to us her creative energy. Indeed all of us became, if not artists, individuals driven by creativity. The vision at the center of the art in this place was in the business, the decor, Christmas preparation, conversation and storytelling. It was in the laughter, the aromas, the money, the beauty and the love. And as my Father once said to me as I struggled to hold on to the legacy of this place in my own troubled life — "One thing I know about you, Martha Ann, you will die trying."

Eye disease is prevalent in my family. I first became aware of this when vision trouble surfaced for my two grandmothers, Grandmother Letterman and Grandmother Benson. Both of these women suffered eye trouble that resulted in the progressive loss of vision in their final years. Once this began, neither of them ever regained their sight.

I was geographically closest to my Grandmother Letterman, so I was able to see how this loss impacted every area of her life. What I most remember, and am astonished by, is that no matter how dim her vision became, it never changed her enthusiasm or her willingness to press forward with her artistic work.

My Grandmother Letterman started her work life as a seamstress. Growing up in poverty, she toiled hard to make her way. She began by sewing garments for the wives of politicians and swiftly attracted attention in these circles. She gained a reputation for her finishing work, and was sought after for this and for related design talents. She always sewed, but it was in her later years that she returned to it as a practice. This occurred when the Tourist Home was gone. She then took it up again, with an energy to rival her early life's efforts.

It was at this time she made dresses of all descriptions for various occasions, mostly, I confess, for me. Among these designs were two of the prettiest dresses I ever owned. They were evening gowns. One was fashioned of emerald green taffeta with spaghetti straps, a finishing bow and with a gold brocade bolero jacket. The other gown was red taffeta with a set of rhinestone shoulder straps. With both of these I wore my first faux fur evening jacket, which she bought for me on the fifth floor at Julius Garfinckel's downtown branch.

At one point during this period of sewing and design extravagance, she made a series of mini skirts for me . . . I could tell she did not really approve of these styles but she had such enjoyment with what was popular, and such a sense of humor, that she went with the trends in the spirit of the times.

In my college years, we had a shawl business. Well, she had one. She made the shawls and sent them to me in great big cardboard boxes. They were crocheted into small and large-scale rectangular and triangular shapes in every color and texture you could even think of. Made of wool, angora, string, or metallic thread, they were gorgeous creations which I sold to fellow students. It seemed, at a certain point, that everyone I knew had at least two of these.

When I finished college, and no longer had an audience for the shawls, my grandmother turned her sights, now significantly dimmed, to crocheting large-scale bed quilts. These, when finished, would be covered with dozens of rosettes and were edged all around with three-inch fringe. These were masterpieces.

As the story goes, her road to success began with a long walk from rural Virginia into the world of Washington, DC. My Grandmother Letterman, first as a seamstress, then as a business woman, and then in her last entrepreneurial ventures with the beautiful stoles and the lace bed coverings, had vision.

It was as if, in the end, light bored her a keyhole, so she was able, with the last borrowed flicker of illumination, to see through what she had been born to do. This was to start and to finish her life as an artist, even if it meant making lace blind.

The Old Homestead

Near 21st and F streets, there is an old driveway entrance. It is located halfway down the block on the left hand side of 21st street as you travel towards E Street. The driveway itself is composed of large and smooth pebbles and small stone chips in cement. Its flecks of mica and granite lend a sparkling aspect. These are actually the remains of an old vehicular entrance that used to travel along the back of the Tourist Home, reaching all the way to 20th Street. That is, until they tore down the great houses that stood between the Empire Apartments and The Tourist Home on F to erect The Statesman Apartments.

The fragments of the old driveway still exist. They are now cracked, raised up, and incomplete. In those days, they sloped up alongside the dark red steps of a Georgian townhome, which I was given at the age of five. It was never used much, as most of the available attention was paid to the three-story houses around the corner on F Street. Visiting this house was like going to the country. Its rooms were furnished well enough, but even then, it seemed like the tail end of a story, rather than a new beginning.

This solitary house soldiered on and had a brief resurgence before its eventual demise in 1963. This occurred when my Aunt Betty was banished from the main block of homes for the sins of her "affair" with Mr. Wink. This was indeed an "elephant in our living rooms." The whole family disapproved. This was a Victorian scandal, to be sure. After all, Aunt Betty was old enough to know better. What kind of example did this set for the children, et cetera, et cetera, et cetera! And—she had responsibilities in the main houses. It just didn't seem right for a scarlet woman to occupy these posts. It set the stage for unhealthy gossiping. But our Aunt Betty seemed unphased. She was happy with her new friend and accepted exile to my house around the corner.

Sometimes when I was lured out to the back of the main homes, with curiosity or by the pull of the fences inhabited by hundreds of fragrant roses in all colors, I would see my Aunt Betty in her pale yellow, white and brown house dress, with her straw funeral fan, cooling herself in the sultry downtown DC humidity. She and her Mr. Wink would "set out there" (as they said in those days) in the melon green metal chairs with the three-quarter-inch square-cut holes, rocking back and forth with the shared joy of happiness found late.

I never visited them any closer than this backyard. They shared their lives until they died in the 1970s. Aunt Betty was the first of our family to go.

When the Tourist Home was sold, Betty and Mr. Wink moved around the corner to the York Apartments. Through the years, this art deco building, which still stands today, housed members of my family in transition. My mother and father lived there for the first year-and-a-half of their marriage. They stayed until February of 1949 when they moved to the Northwest neighborhood of Spring Valley into our first family home on Corey Place, where my story began.

I do not think any of us recovered from the sale and subsequent demolition of the Tourist Home. Only a few of us remain who actually remember, and we, to a one, are haunted. Or at least, until now, I have been. With the specter of the long wall of aromatic roses and to its left the parade of listing porches with screen doors flung wide, I am often drawn into the memory of the atmosphere of that unforgettable family enterprise, and of old DC, to be comforted and to remember.

Cigar Smoke

It permeated the establishment. It was on every floor. It was at the desk, in the lobbies and parlors, in the dining rooms, and in the vestibules. It was part of the place. This aroma was the scent of my Grandfather Letterman.

There was also the related paraphernalia, the lighters, the books of matches, the cigar boxes, the ash trays, and very often a trail of the ashes themselves. My Grandfather favored the El Producto Brand but would smoke many varieties. We would venture out into Foggy Bottom to buy these cigars at Quigley's Drug Store and we got to keep many of the cigar boxes. All of the aspects of the Tourist Home went together symphonically and this was the bass fiddle, its low notes underscoring the atmosphere. The smoke brought with it connections to Grandfather's other world. He was an official on the Metropolitan Police Department of the District of Columbia during the era of prohibition and served until the '60s when he retired. During his career, he served as a vice-squad captain leading many successful raids. I knew nothing of this at the time but could sense something of it as a child.

As I grew older, I became impatient with Grandfather's smoking his cigars. I thought the habit was messy and inappropriate to the tenor of the establishment. Never mind that this was his house. This was none of my business.

Before the Tourist Home was torn down, the furniture began to disappear, and what was being saved was moved to a high pile in the lobby of the house on the corner of 21st and F, rising to the ceiling like a funeral pyre.

The aroma of the cigars, the perfume, and the food stuck to the walls, the rugs, our ribs, and our hearts. As the structures were torn away from us, almost the only thing to cling to was that whisper of the past, pungently punctuating the air, as if to offer an anchor. It gave back to us the empty rooms and lobbies, and kitchens, and halls, and stairways, until finally, holding on for dear life, all that was left for us as we inhaled, was the sting of our tears as we gazed out upon the emptiness.

The Recurring Dream

I no longer have the recurring dream. I believe, at some point, I just gave up, because I knew that, waking or sleeping, this particular one was impossible.

My dream always began the same way. It was 1964. I was alone, in the last lobby of the Tourist Home in Foggy Bottom, in Washington, DC. I stood there in the room with the high pile of furniture that was ready to be moved to our own house or to my grandparents' temporary apartment across the street. Save for this pile, and the furniture ready to be auctioned off, the remaining houses and lobbies were deserted in preparation for the coming demolition.

I walked up the stairs to the first landing at 2020 to look over the towering assembly of these pieces of our lives. Suddenly, I could feel the swirled burgundy carpet beneath my feet. Its dizzying patterns, spiraling and turning me to the next flight of stairs. I would take them one at a time, noticing everything: A hint of perfume (more than a hint), the aroma of cigar and cigarette smoke, the heavy air of abandoned buildings all around. Beckoned by the light from the second floor spilling from the now unlocked, open doors of our guest rooms, I would enter each room to look at the discarded furniture.

Here were the beds with their mattresses, once graced with the heavy chenille bedspreads, now bare—a fading memory. There were patches of darker flooring, where the rugs and area carpets had lain. There were old bureaus and chests of drawers, rocking chairs, wall sconces, and discolored patches of paint on the walls where pictures had hung. There were the corner sinks in the rooms with no private baths, with their mirrors and medicine cabinets above, or the private baths with the art deco features. There were great painted wardrobe closets, and blanket chests, chairs and small side tables. In the rooms were roll-away beds and lamps of all sizes, figural and plain. There were wicker and metal porch chairs and gliders on the outside porches, which themselves were tilting. Hanging tentatively in the air, they would whisper to me, "Please don't make us go away! Can we not stay a little while longer? Where is John? Where is Georgie? Have you seen Betty or Jack? Maybe Mr. Wink would help us. Perhaps, you could ask again, just to be certain it is true. Is it our fault things turned out this way?"

I would have this same experience, varying only slightly, from room, to room, to room. Sometimes I would make it all the way up to the third floor, with its small, stark chambers. Sometimes not. Often I would collapse in my favorite suite, at the end of the second floor hall, on its porch at the back, in one of the daybeds. I would look up at the bead-board ceiling, wondering . . . What will we do now? Where will we go? What is to become of all of this, of us?

No Sunday dinners, no wardrobes to climb into to dream of Narnia, no air filled with the scent of home, no conversation spilling through the cracks in the walls, no plaster friezes to witness our follies or our celebrations of new life, no whole rooms filled with Santa's workshop, waiting to be delivered through the crisp night skies of holiday winter, no humid outdoor rooms full of spun tales, no transient visitors, no permanent residents—now an extension of our family—to witness and to add to the whole of the story. No, in these moments, I would not make it to the third floor.

But, when sleep took me far enough under its wing, I would make it to the top. Then I would look out of the tiny windows in the corner rooms, or if in the hall again, crane my neck, turning my gaze up at the skylight in the high ceiling, suddenly exclaiming—"Ah!" and, transfixed, ask, "Did I make it? Is this heaven? Did they let me go, too? Please! Let that be it!"

Of, course, that was not it.

Soon enough, reality would bleed through the dreamscape. Earthbound once more, I would take my final tour of the corridors, wandering in the disappearance of our history, storing everything I could in a heart already filled with the memory of this home.

Over time, I never got back there. The dream became shorter and shorter until all that I could recall would surface in a daydream or in a flash-flood of tears.

A young girl stood alone in the center of a hall in
the last house, fragments of crystalline memory rendering
dust motes, a waterfall of glitter sifting through the air,
falling like silver snow, burying her in a gentle coat of light,
a mantle of everything, a train worn into the night.
She was transformed—a diva—full of song, and the
memory of it all became her new secret, a silent aria.

Mustard Seed

"If you have faith like a grain of mustard seed, you will
say to this mountain, 'Move from here to there,' and it
will move, and nothing will be impossible for you."

Matthew 17:20 – English Standard Version

The mustard seed was the first charm on my gold charm bracelet.
I had a bracelet in silver, as well, but the gold one was the centerpiece
of my charm jewelry collection.

As I see it now, of all of the occasions and golden tokens I was
given to mark them, the mustard seed, with the little opalescent dome
covering it, seems the most significant. I do not believe I realized it at
the time, but this gift was chosen from the point of view of a resilient,
strong family faith. This hovered as an awareness. Only now do I see
that it was a kernel central to my history. This kept me alive and
hopeful, no matter what the circumstances, and had me embracing
the wilds of a creative spirit. Saddest of all were the times when I
would wander past the barriers of this faith, looking for what I already
possessed, only to find a wasteland, inside and out.

This must have been when the grief took over—and the wandering.
There is a tribe, really, of people who keep their pain close, like a
precious secret not to be told. You always know when you have met
one of their number. It is somewhere, just behind the eyes, under
lowered lids, and an almost imperceptible sinking of the shoulders.
This is a heaviness that does not go with anything outside of this
brand of aching.

As I grow older, I am less and less able to bear these feelings alone.
So I am writing it all down before I die, so that I can pull up and expel
the memories that are attached to the deep red rose beauty of my life
and to the coal darkness of it, and in the cinders rendered, place
before my audience the pieces of the puzzle. I am hoping that in laying
bare my story, with its twists and turns, its alleyways of despair, and its
mountains of hope, there will be a mirror held up to another's life.

Atlantic City

Atlantic City

The Atlantic City Skyline

I traveled to Atlantic City with my grandparents. By the time we reached the Atlantic City Expressway, anticipation flared up, and each one of us, in his or her own style, would prepare for what was ahead. It was just one more mile, we told ourselves. This was when we began to look for signs.

Indeed, first to come were the billboards, which, everywhere along the route, were depicting what we looked forward to: hotels, piers, sun worshipping, theatrical and musical entertainments, and restaurants. The images floated high above our heads and over the land bordering the roads beckoning us forward to the horizon we longed for. Now, we really were closer. The landscape itself lent us its composition like a clue. Our road passed over wet marshes, glistening pools of water, and soon after, grasses and soft patches of earth. Shifting sands skittered across the road forming designs that we would interrupt, first with the tires of our cars, and later with those of the larger scale buses.

Then all of a sudden, it was there, the Atlantic City skyline. A wild lineup of buildings in all shapes and sizes, appearing out of absolutely nowhere, a fantastic explosion of castles in the wetlands.

We, among the thousands of others, arrived at the seaside, took possession of our rooms, put on our finery, and went forth to that old world "meet up" to play our parts in the grandest of all operas, the one that took place in our imaginations on the Atlantic City boardwalk. In this city, "The Queen of Resorts," we felt like royalty and we all turned in unison in lines that stretched for miles to face the wide open sea, watching wave after wave crash onto the beach, and move toward us, as if we were receiving visitors and dignitaries to our lavish, golden, neon-flashing, sun-struck court.

Arrivals

We arrived by train, by car, by limousine and, in the final years, by Trailways and Greyhound bus. It did not matter that the train service was discontinued, or that my Grandfather no longer drove the stylish black Cadillac, or that the limousine service became too extravagant. We were not proud. We did what had to be done. As we left our home for the street, hailed a Yellow or Diamond cab, and went down to the old terminal on New York Avenue in Washington, DC, we knew one thing only: we had to get to Atlantic City.

When we reached the shore depot, where the old trains used to come in, we took a taxi to our beloved hotel, the Claridge. Once we had crossed the entrance on Indiana Avenue, it was as if we had arrived still in the style of our most luxurious conveyance. The doorman may have noticed, but we were never made to feel small by the obvious change in our circumstances. A palpable sense of dignity characterized these arrivals at the "Skyscraper by the Sea."

As with many of my other mental souvenirs, I can, with a moment to lower my head, recall Atlantic City as it was some fifty years ago. So that, as I look up, I am 16 years old in my summer dress of black polka dots with the voile collar, and the patent leather handbag and matching shoes. I am emerging from the taxi, the car, or the limousine, followed by my Grandfather Letterman in his summer weight suit, his straw hat and his wingtip spectator shoes. My Grandmother Letterman emerges last, but not least, in her Kelly green dress, her white summer weight sweater over her shoulders, and her own matching black patent leather pocketbook and heels. She is wearing Emeraude by Coty and loose face powder is falling from her cheeks onto the front of her dress like volcano ash. I am wearing Ambush by Dana, hoping for an honorable mention from the bellman.

The heavy brass, glass, and steel double doors were held open for us. There were four sets of these across the front of the building. Once indoors, the elegant flow of deluxe service awaited as we proceeded to the registration desk to begin our highly anticipated stay.

The Oceanfront Rooms

For me, the best part of a room with an ocean view was that I could open the window to let the breeze in, which would cause the curtains to float into the chamber. I suppose it was normal to want this. I came to expect this good fortune and comfort. Of course, eventually these windows were replaced and sealed off. I am guessing this was done for purposes of temperature control as much as from a growing fear that people would step off the ledges. Whatever the reasons, the small rooms today, now fully modernized and tastefully restored, lack the haunting poetry of the sea music I once experienced from within their confines.

In those lovely old days, there was a spirit to the whole place that fed me even as I slept or napped in my bed. And it seemed that was provided by a simple window, which once opened, became a gateway for a refreshing greeting from the air of the sea.

The Transoms

They were high flying rectangles of light. I sent through these, to the winds, all of the imprisoning despair that I had brought with me. These were feelings that did not match this time of respite. For this week alone, I vowed I would be free, parking all preoccupations outside the room in the breeze filled hallway. This small shape, lifting toward hope, floated—like a promise—over the shuttered door of our hotel room, as if it was crafted just to ventilate my uncertainty.

Some might see this tiny window as a useless detail, but it was one of a myriad of architectural details that made Atlantic City the place I loved.

Breakfast at the Skyscraper by the Sea

We began our days at the New Jersey seashore with breakfast at the Claridge Hotel, the vintage 1930s "Skyscraper by the Sea." The dining room was one circular staircase flight up from the mezzanine level. I liked to approach it from this direction. Like arriving in Venice, Italy, by boat, it was the only way to arrive.

In attendance, most often, were my Grandmother and Grandfather Letterman and me. We always had a lovely table positioned in a window overlooking the terrace, and below in Brighton Park, the "Fountain of Light."

I believe Grandmother must have tipped the service professionals handsomely, because we were always greeted and seated preferentially.

The breakfast menu was made of paper in a shiny heavy stock and had the dining selections printed inside in blue ink. These offerings were laid out on the pages in neat and easy to understand categories. The feeling of this menu, as presented, was playful. There were colorful images on the cover in a style that was both cartoonish and elegant.

We would arrive at tables beautifully set with tablecloths and toppers of paper place mats at each seat. I loved these and would usually request an extra to take home as a souvenir. Butter was on the table in silver-plated bowls of shaved ice, next to baskets of Melba toast. As we took our seats, our water glasses were instantly filled by the busboys in their white uniforms. The wait staff wore dark green trousers and tangerine colored jackets. All of the uniforms were perfectly pressed and formally crisp. Where in the world the hotel had enough people to do all of that laundry and dry cleaning, I cannot begin to imagine. The staff was composed of efficient, kind, and amusing characters of every nationality and ethnicity.

The meals they served were chosen from the playful little menu and were absolutely NOT playful. I think they wanted you to imagine this was a breezy seaside repast, masquerading somehow, the real truth of the bacon, eggs, sausages, ham, hominy, pancakes, hash browns, biscuits, gravy, and steak that were actually placed in front of us. Oh, all right sometimes we had a fruit cup and a bowl of Cream of Wheat, oatmeal, or dry cereal, but it was mostly, from the beginning, creamed chipped beef, creamed chicken, cream cheese, creamy anything that made its way from the tableside trolley to our smacking lips. We lingered for an hour or so over the early meals before retiring to our rooms to prepare for shopping excursions and snacks on the boardwalk.

The sound of early morning was the ever-present music of the sea. This was the backdrop for silverware clinking against china plates, and spoons stirring milk and sugar into coffee and tea cups.*

The feeling in the room was one of ease and grandeur. Not that we were particularly, any of us, grand, or at our ease.

But . . .

We were all pretending that we were. It was exquisitely choreographed personal theatre, executed from the first moments of dining in the morning, to those lasting long into our dreams in the middle of the night.

* *Filled from the steaming hottles*
  that teemed with our beverages.

Luncheon at The Meri Mayfair Lounge

Never mind that we had just eaten breakfast two hours prior, or that our morning walk down the boardwalk had featured some of the wonderful flavors of Fralinger's salt water taffy. We were at the beach. I do not care how dainty the two-inch pieces looked in their individual wrappers, with the twisted tied ends. It was still sugar and we were buzzing like bees by the time we approached the glamorous luncheon lounge.

When I was small, this room seemed like a salon in a grand hotel. True enough, it was luxurious, but in the Claridge Hotel where the average guest room was 90 square feet, the afternoon dining salon was really only three times that size. We were always greeted and served with aplomb. We never felt rushed but did understand that everyone wanted a turn.

Upon entering the burgundy, black, and silver room, which at any time of day seemed to be alive, one instantly felt the romance. It was like being in an old time movie. I had the impression that many celebrated individuals passed through its doors, and now knowing who they actually were, I realize that my intuition was correct.

I knew, with every passing year of my childhood, the time would come when I could approach the room in the nightclub hours. That story was just beginning and I really never did get a full adult pass at its evenings. That is just as well.

Entering through the heavy glass doors, we immediately passed chafing dishes with seafood and vegetables and other delectable warming entrees. However, our meals began with cocktails, a Whisky Sour or Old Fashioned for my Grandmother, scotch or bourbon for my Grandfather, and a Shirley Temple with extra cherry for me. The service was accommodating but brisk. This luncheon seating, wedged between the two grand presentations of the first and last meals of the day, had a special atmosphere—a style of its own. There was always something held in reserve.

We were never left wanting, but the air of mystery seemed to hold memories of the past and a feeling of anticipation for what was coming. We were caught in this odd limbo. We ordered our sole and flounder, our side dishes, and desserts, and, bit by bit, we outgrew our clothing, because none of us could resist eating the delicious food.

But . . .

In The Meri Mayfair Lounge, it was glamour, front and center, that we feasted upon and would try to relive for years to come.

The Beach Chairs and the Umbrellas

There we were, at the head of the stairs on the boardwalk. Just below these twenty steps, or so, waited the gentlemen who rented the beach chairs and umbrellas to us. They would also deliver them to our chosen spot on the sand. They had a way, with their strength and muscular builds, to spear the sand with the pointed umbrella poles. Single handed, they could bury them deep enough to withstand a stiff breeze from the ocean.

These men would also remain to set up the deck chairs and could arrange for cabanas, if need be. This was not cheap but was worth it, for all sorts of reasons. Any way you chose to approach the beach, these men and their wares awaited. The shade of the umbrella, the comfort of the chairs, we needed it all, we especially appreciated Randy, Bucky and Tom. The accommodation and attractiveness of the shore staff were all part of the experience. The brilliant colors of red, blue, green, and yellow striped canvas stood out against the blue background of the ocean. It felt like we were living in a fairy-tale sand castle. The experience was fragile, in one moment rising to the sky, the next, swept out to sea—.

The Beach Vendors

High above, red advertisements trailed behind the small rumbling aircraft in the blue skies of Atlantic City, New Jersey. There we were, lying in a stupor on the sand at two o'clock in the afternoon. We had finished our breakfast, lunch, and our snacks from on and under the boardwalk. My grandparents and I were now listening to the music of the vendors who were selling their wares on the beach. These boys were seashore trademarks. We looked forward to seeing them and hearing the sound of their voices as they called out their offerings. "Ice cream here, ice-cold ice cream!" These sellers wore silver boxes slung over their shoulders like giant pocketbooks. And from inside those steaming beds of dry ice, they sold wonderful ice cream and cold treats.

With the backdrop of the roaring ocean, the squealing of children playing in the water and building sand castles, the high pitched whistles of the life guards (also very attractive), this seemed to be a "cool" summer job for what appeared to be an army of adolescents.

I now realize those professionals were part of a vast and complex business machine running Atlantic City, and that nothing, no matter how serendipitous or casual it may have seemed at the time, was offered without very careful orchestration.

Atlantic City had always been a place of layered existences and realities. There was forever a constant shimmer—of something mysterious, alluring and dangerous. Today, I am glad the experience I had was in the societal fantasy instead of the place where it was engineered.

Washing Our Feet

We stayed until at least 3:30 pm. This allowed us a half hour to get back to our accommodations to avail ourselves of the traditional, luxurious, afternoon, open-windowed, sea-breeze nap time.

The route we took from the beach went up the wooden stairs of the boardwalk, then across the expanse of steaming planks to a ramp that led to the street. This disembarkation point was just under the famous, second floor Needlecraft Salon (an establishment catering to the design and fashion needs of wealthy and often quite famous patrons). The walkway was flat and went straight ahead, and then it sloped to the street below, to the right hand side of the central fountain situated in Brighton Park—the manicured gardens in front of the Claridge Hotel. We walked along the sidewalk until we reached the new building that had replaced the rambling old Brighton Hotel. Only then did we cross the street to our entrance portico. We then headed sharply to the right to walk along the side of the building.

Sometimes, in remembering, I retrace my steps, following this route, arriving, as in the older days, at the side door that served as an exit and reentry for, among others, the resort's swimmers and sun worshippers. Just outside this service door, I notice the old water spout. This is where we, upon returning from the beach, would be obliged to wash our feet. Normally this activity would take just a sprinkle or two. In our case it took longer, because the sands of these beaches had a fine consistency and contained many tiny granules of black that would stick to our sun oiled skin like glue. I must admit that we cheated a bit in this practice. By now we were relaxed, full of food, and the fun of our exertions. In our haste to make short work of the ritual washing, I am certain we left a grainy trail as we returned to our rooms on the upper floors.

Sometimes, when I happen upon the water faucet from my youth, I hesitate to linger, but remark to myself as I go on my way, that, if it had been possible, I would have removed my shoes to wash my feet once more from this spout, until the river of my thoughts from those old, warm, ocean air days returned to me.

Hot and Cold, Fresh and Salt Water Bathing

Thick pink enamel, white shower curtains, signature hotel bath towels and mats, and hot and cold running fresh and salt water from four individual spigots were available to us when we took our bathing pleasure at the Claridge Hotel in Atlantic City, New Jersey. Coming back from the beach, I would choose to use the flowing salt water coming in from the ocean. I wanted to prolong the experience and sooth myself with its lingering aroma before nap time.

These bathrooms were small, but well appointed, with sturdy enamel tubs and sinks. Features of extra comfort were soft, ample bath robes, special soaps from the Claridge Hotel and a plenitude of steaming water for cleansing and relaxation.

Such was the simplicity and complete satisfaction of one rare old custom from "back in the day."

Letter Writing

In every room there was a desk with a blotter, a lamp, and a comfortable chair. Also, the hotel provided a selection of embossed papers and envelopes for use in writing letters to friends and acquaintances. I would augment these using collections of picture postcards purchased from the hotel concession stand and souvenir shops on the boardwalk.

Writing letters from Atlantic City was a chief pastime. It was important to me, and it was in these short missives that I would attempt to capture the spirit and experience of the place and to share my discoveries.

It also provided time for reverie and contemplation. Life was slower then. The means of communication were limited and were not immediately gratifying. Eager to share these special days, I wrote, sent, and waited—wondering how my news would be received, and in this pursuit, I discovered that the stillness and reflection were part of the glory of it all.

Dressing for Dinner

It was a ritual. I believe that added to the appeal. It began after the relaxing afternoon nap, which was a rite all of its own. Decisions needed to be made about clothing, jewelry and shoes. Most certainly, an effort needed to be made to plan what Grandfather would wear for the evening.

We chose our outfits with care because they had to last through the walk to the dining room, the dining event itself, and the nightly trip to the boardwalk. Our ensembles usually included a suitable wrap to later ward off the chilly evening air. Having packed very carefully for our trip, we had many items from which to choose.

I especially enjoyed this daily creative time. It was a delicious luxury to sort through finery, as if it were candy, in order to carefully select just the right flavor for the coming occasions. And then the "donning of apparel" and the accessorizing. Being a child for many of my years in Atlantic City, my "grown-up" pleasure came from helping my Grandmother dress and from dipping into her sartorial larder for details to add spirit to my own girlish clothing. These were usually from a collection of scarves and jewelry that featured everything from rhinestone earrings, crystal and glass bead necklaces, to pop-it beads.

Last, but not least, came makeup and fragrance. I would take great delight in watching my Grandmother as she applied lipstick, powder, rouge and what she called "toilet water." Remembering some of the examples of the latter, I am inclined to understand the term. Whatever the outcome of her eccentric costume and cosmetic regime, the process and fun of dressing for dinner, especially in the realm of finishing touches, was from beginning to end, marvelous and ridiculous.

I will forever be grateful for this balance. We three were earnestly interested in the smallest details that gave us pleasure. Many of these customs and pastimes were part of a vast fabric of life that was dying out as fast as we could partake of adding to its detail. All that remains in its wake is a heavy grief for a lost beauty of thought, word, and deed.

Dinner at the Claridge Hotel

It was in the same room where, hours before, we had broken our fast (as if we ever stopped eating).

But . . . it was not the same room, somehow.

We arrived at the entrance, using the sweeping spiral staircase route. Now, clad in our evening attire, we felt like featured performers in the lowering light of the disappearing sun. Perhaps we imagined it, but the entrances we made seemed enhanced by our sparkling accessories and by the brilliant crystal chandeliers and wall sconces. We received the light as though we were being announced and glided into the room following the leads of the Maître d' and the head waiter.

We were ushered though tables that seemed to be bathed in a sea of soft pink linen. The napkins, sitting like pastel mountain peaks, hinted at the heights of pleasure we might reach during the next hours of dining. The atmosphere of the salon at night was decidedly "cocktail." The music was provided by the hotel's intimate chamber trios and quartets. The sound came from everywhere, a classical sound, ebbing and flowing with the conversations, to accompany the classic luxury of our hotel.

The evening menus were lavish and larger than the breezy morning menu. The staff was dressed elegantly for the evening. The Maître d' wore an off white or a pale blue dinner jacket. The head waiter wore dark green, and the wait staff were suited in white uniforms trimmed in burgundy cloth with gold buttons. They all wore black trousers.

The dining salon windows overlooking the spectacular "Fountain of Light" were suffused with the glow of the room's fixtures and reflected the images we presented to each other and to the world as we gathered in the sumptuous, glittering hall for dinner. The carpet was patterned and plush. It welcomed our feet, in their expensive shoes, to its perpetual comfort and beauty.

Once we were seated, the drinks came. My Grandmother ordered her Whisky Sour or Old Fashioned, my Grandfather had his bourbon, and I had my Shirley Temple. Now we were set. Upright in our chairs, sipping our beverages, we waited to be counted in. We did not really know any of the guests at the adjacent tables. It was up to each family to bring its own entourage. Some years we did. Then my brother, my sister, my parents, or my aunts and cousins would join us.

I was a young girl, living in a troubled home, and my grandparents were servants to their guests in the hospitality industry. So here we were, free for one week, and we all wanted something different. We were stewards of our brief imaginary territories and were tended by kind individuals, who seemed happy to respond to our relatively modest requests.

No, it was not real, but it was so full a world, that the strings of the chamber harps and cellos seemed to be those of our own hearts, and that was *before* we ordered the FOOD.

The Fountain of Light

No matter how it was approached, the "Fountain of Light" was pure magic. Under any circumstances, when operating in rainbow color, it could be heard. Through the opened windows in my hotel room, I could lie in bed after a full day of "The Queen of Resorts" and listen to its music. With the constant rising and falling of water, there was a scintillating movement to the sound, both powerful and haunting.

The reality of the fountain's light was stunning. Just as the millions of bulbs that now illuminate the world, this water garden became a symbol of the future with its tall sprays of red, yellow, green, and white showering the sky.

In the old days, my favorite way to hear this music was to sit at the corner table of the Claridge Hotel dining room with the terrace's french windows open to the evening for its ever-present song. It made me feel, when I heard or saw it, that its lights were inextinguishable and its music permanent. After dinner, I would walk toward these shimmering waters as if to be baptized for the coming engagement with high society at the sea shore.

Our Walks Down the Earth

The Boardwalk.

Once I was introduced to the remarkable surface of the Atlantic City Boardwalk, I belonged there. Whether I approached it from the beach, from the city streets, or from the frothy undertow of the ocean, I felt welcomed. It was like arriving upon a stage. Walking on the boardwalk was a dance.

There were thousands of us with the same dream—to be all we hoped we could be. A tall order—but, once a year, on a stage perfectly set for the glamour and luxury of our play, anything seemed possible, especially at night. This was when we chose our evening attire and went on parade.

For me, time passed too quickly. My summer stays occurred between the years of 1951–1968. As for my grandparents, they began in the 1930s. Every year at the same time in August, Atlantic City offered total immersion in a dream.

At the time, I think I believed it all to be true. In my mind, we were rich, lovely beyond measure, and without a care in the world. I thought I was entitled to beauty, and the motion of it, and I expected the regal scope of my life to be there forever. And it was, for a time, until it, like all of the rest of what I called home, disappeared.

Only now do I realize the responsibility for beauty in the dance on earth is my own. And that whatever circumstances life brings, I have a choice to move with dignity and grace, or not. I have a choice to do it big, beautiful and brave, or small, half finished, and hidden from the world.

Mr. Peanut

I believe we all have some greater being or sense of something outside of ourselves that guides us. I have this faith. I also know there must have been, along my way, other, less serious, but important in their own way, guides. These could take the form of people, things, imaginary or real places, or more playful images of kindly helpers. One playful helper was present for me during all the summers of my youth and early adult life. He rotated physically, high above my head, turning, turning with an always-ready smile, and a jauntiness of step. He swiveled aloft, as if roasting on a spit, basted almost, with salty air, popcorn, fudge, taffy, cotton candy, the smell of the boardwalk, and expensive or very cheap, fabulously romantic perfume.

He nodded graciously, wrapped in his own irreplaceable fragrance, dancing and tipping his hat, as if to say, "You, my dear, are today, tonight, and forever on a blessed path of your own. Should you ever doubt it, remember me in the sunlight, the mists of fog, or in bright, starry, neon night. Remember me circling above you with my happy face. I believe in you, as you once, with all of the innocence of your youth, took me to heart. Now, it is my turn. I shall dance with you. I will walk to your side with my long thin black cane, offer my arm, and step out with you."

And when we pass other couples, they will quietly nod and smile and tip their own hats and their dainty parasols to wave us understandingly on. They will exclaim in surprise in our wake saying . . . "Well, Did You Ever? There goes Martha Ann with Mr. Peanut! I do declare!"

What a Pair!

Kewpie Doll

This was a fragile playmate. She crinkled in my small hands like cellophane and cracked egg shells. She was cheerful and colorful with her bright, feathery costume of hot pink, orange, lime green, and lemon yellow. Sometimes there were tiny decorative jewels for the embellishment of her minute outfit.

My Grandfather Letterman won her for me in the bustling, noisy aisles of the Million Dollar Pier. I named her Susie. She was, in spite of her size, just grand, with her sunny disposition, bowed lips, big eyes, and light-weight prettiness. After all of the games and amusements we enjoyed, I ferried her back to my hotel room to make a bed for her in my train case.

At our vacation's end, she came home with me to Washington, DC to the more subdued blues, burgundies, browns, and beiges of our residential palette. She was a soothing match for me, with her faint movements and sounds of life. I let the comfort of her cheer me on through the seasons of my year, until our next summer came, and we could again visit the amusement pier that was her first home.

I cherished her friendship, and she carried my brittle heart in the days of our lives together. She was my carnival Kewpie Doll.

Room Service

We knew it had arrived, even before we heard it—the knock at the door. First, we were waiting for it, and second, we saw the waiter through the slanting shutters of our doorway. Room service always made us feel special. Who knows what possessed us to order more food when we had already consumed three meals and snacks, but it did not prevent us from calling in our desires for MORE.

Sometimes we would order the traditional club sandwich with Coca-Cola. But, most often, we would order sherbet with vanilla ice cream, light cookies, and tea. This would arrive on a rolling cart in silver-plated iced bowls filled with vanilla, lemon with vanilla, orange with vanilla, or lime with vanilla and wafer-thin cookies placed on top. We would just sit, propped up, or lay flat on our backs, and spoon in these delicate sweets.

"Hello, this is Martha Letterman from room 86 calling for my Grandmother Letterman. She would like to order . . . " and I would relay. I was also in charge, when the treats arrived, of the tip.

There was something luxurious in these proceedings. The customs and rituals we observed were what we had wanted and now treasured.

Especially my grandparents, who had their own hotel, and whose every waking day involved serving and caring for others. This was their time and I was then, and I am today, in memoir, one of their chief, and most ardent, witnesses.

The Violin Serenades

The Hotel Claridge featured violin trios and quartets during the dinner seating. The music was so beautifully played that the first bowed strings carried a life-changing sound that crossed a bridge to someplace deep within myself. As a young girl, I did not know how this sound would apply in my life but I knew I had received a message, and that it had made a strong impression.

The violin solo I heard that evening was played at our tableside by a member of the hotel dining room's instrumental ensemble. It was a surprisingly romantic moment and it felt tailor-made for me. I am certain it was not, but I remembered it. Later on I learned it was an aria from the German opera *Martha*.

Well . . .

What I could not have known at the time was that these dining rooms and their adjacent salons provided homes for regular performances of the touring Metropolitan Opera. The music, and the memory of music, were permanent fixtures in these halls. It was almost as if the pathways between the tables were filled with specters of Faust, Cio-Cio-San, Marguerite, Suzuki, Dorabella, Fiordiligi, Susanna, Rosina, Doctor Bartolo, Lt. B. F. Pinkerton, Violetta, Germont, Barbarina, counts and countesses, kings and queens, princesses and fairy dust. These shadow figures became my family.

Over the years, as I grew in maturity and experience, I was given the chance to bring them, some anyway, to life on the stage. This was not so difficult to manage, really, as they had moved in and out of my thinking for years. I discovered that I knew their movements as well as my own.

So it was that I became an opera director, ushered into my career by the sound of a violin solo whose beautiful strings had called my name.

The Ice Capades

Right from the start, there were bittersweet aspects to going to the Ice Capades at the old Atlantic City Convention Hall. First, it was an event that we attended at the conclusion of our week at the beach in August. Second, we costumed ourselves and arrived by limousine, so it was a bit removed from our routine. Third, the event itself held elements of all that we aspired to be, but had not yet, or never would, become. It was beautifully staged, visually opulent, magnificent mobile theatre.

When the performance was over, we walked back to our hotel with the aromas of roasting peanuts, popcorn, salt water taffy, cotton candy, french fried potatoes and creosote presented to us like the top notes of a perfume.

I do not think we were shy about our wistfulness, as we all felt it, and we always shared the full complement of our feelings on our trips to the sea. The emotions were part of it.

The ice dancing itself was, as it was executed by the soloists and the couples, intrinsically romantic. It brought all of our own sensibilities to the foreground. I know that seeing all of this poetic movement shaped my sense of motion and music, and led me to an understanding that I would not have had otherwise.

Years later I became a director of plays and of operas. Ideas for movement in theatre were my specialty. I grew to feel that clearly motivated physical expression enhanced performance and reached even closer to an audience. I think it left the performers with a full sense of their capabilities that they drew from deep within.

It seems to me now as though my creativity was being inspired. With each hissing and scraping of the steel blades across the cool ice, a layer of my frozen heart thawed and left me open to the truth of my own creative path.

Cleopatra

Right about the time the 1963 Twentieth Century Fox film *Cleopatra* was released, we began to sense something was not right in Atlantic City, New Jersey. The old rooming houses were being boarded up and were being replaced with motels. The streets behind the boardwalk were suddenly, inexplicably, different. 1950s air travel had lured vacationers to new Caribbean and Florida destinations, causing the great numbers, who had at one time chosen this resort, to diminish.

Atlantic City's Cinema Theater premier of *Cleopatra*, this unprecedented, expensive Hollywood film, seemed also to forecast the end of an illusion-inflated era at the shore. We told ourselves it wasn't true, holding onto our denial, telling ourselves everything would remain the same. If this was not the case, we all wondered . . . Where in the world would we go?

This was important to me, but to my grandparents, who had been made whole by this travel experience since the 1930s . . .

Well . . .

This new loss came as an additional heartbreak.

Going to the doomed movie was no limousine trip to the Ice Capades at the nearby, impressive, convention center. Neither was it a glorious evening in a boardwalk movie palace. This was a trek through the back streets of our desires.

We arrived for the occasion dressed like movie stars, not fully understanding what we were about to witness and feel. Like the ill-fated lovers in our movie, we had stepped closer to an omen of things to come. We still had four more years to frequent our favored resort, but we did not know this either. The movie at the Cinema Theater was five hours long. It was colossal in scope and in disappointment.

As we exited the theatre that evening, our fancy clothing seemed to hang on our frames like rags, our stoles and bejeweled sweaters, wilting over our shoulders, our small pocketbooks, dangling from loose fingers.

I remember, on the long walk back to our hotel, feeling weighted with a dull ache that could not be filled by popcorn and Coca-Cola, or even by being thin. Once ensconced in our comfortable hotel room, not even the familiar ritual of room service could remove the new, palpable, preoccupation and concern.

"The Good Old Days" were going, and they were, we knew for certain, going to take us with them forever.

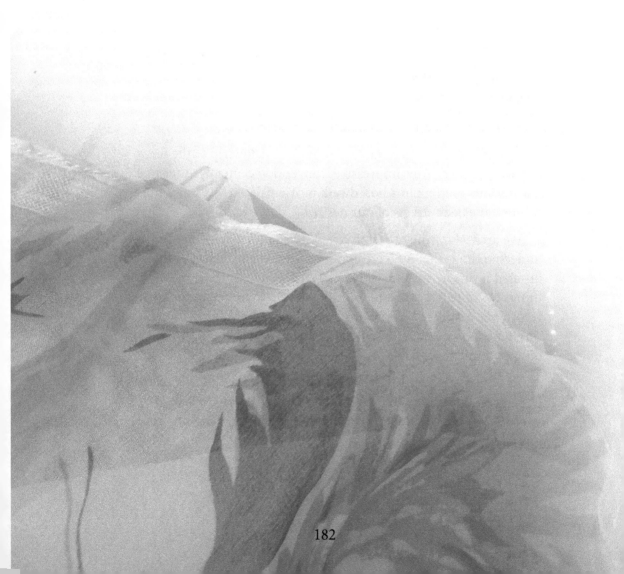

Swizzle Sticks

There were so many, we barely knew where to put them. We settled on the mid-sized salt water taffy box from Fralinger's. Eventually, after sifting through our favorites, we ended up with a tailored collection that could be comfortably housed in one of the smaller proportioned candy boxes. They came in white, gold, silver, pale pink, royal blue, emerald green, yellow, red and clear plastic. They were simple ridged sticks with a little ball on the top. The writing on them was raised in gold and spelled out the Claridge Hotel.

We collected them at our lunch and dinner seatings. They arrived in the mixed drinks, the cocktails and the soft drinks. Over the course of a week, we were able to assemble quite a group of these. They just nestled in their box as a reminder of our stupendous meals and conversations in those days, waving from their cardboard containers like high society banners in one moment or colorful more relaxed images of picket fences bordering our summer escapades in another—like an illusion of "home sweet home."

I loved to lie on the roll-away bed, line them up by color, and count them as if in their nightly increasing numbers they could bring me closer to some picture that was taking shape in my mind. For me, they became, not sticks, but pieces of plastic lumber, with which I could build a house for myself where I could be happy and safe. Where I could decorate and place my pretty things around me. Where no one could come to take them away from me, or tell me I could not keep them. I could just sit there of an evening, on this uneven surface, and construct a place of bright magic until bedtime.

It was then, in that sleepy time, that the pieces of my dream house would collapse and clatter into their own bed in the green, yellow, and brown paper box and wait for the lid to close over their rounded heads for the night. I would turn over on the roll-away for my own sleep, using evening shadows cast on the walls, to over and over again, replay the movie of the dazzling, marching swizzle sticks in their command performances.

Departures

It is hard for me to believe that, when I left Atlantic City in the summer of 1968, I would never again see the world that I had, by then, memorized in my bones as my own. That, as I went to work in summer theatre, and onward to find my way as an independent adult, a vital part of my foundation was crumbling behind my back. By the time I was able or inclined to return to this place of wonder, it had vanished, except for a few well-hidden fragments of its glorious architectural history.

Hotels, which might as well have been cities, were razed, leaving empty lots behind. Where there once had been gardens, terraces, lobbies, dining halls, solariums and kitchens, where there had existed ballrooms that could entertain 4,000 souls at a time, as in the case of the incredible Traymore Hotel, now, there was nothing.

This was not just a loss of grand architecture to the cement, glass, and mirrored towers that took their places. This was a permanent removal of a lifestyle that had been curated for almost a century of people. People, who once they grasped the turn history had taken, had nowhere to go. Now, with only their memories to guide them through the deserted side streets, they try to live in the remains of their disappearing city.

Where once there had been accommodations for all stratas of society, now only derelict and forgotten properties were left. There was no place to be comforted, except at the library, or at shops where images were bound in hundreds of books of postcards and photographs.

These really are some of the only visual blessings still available. Their stewards are angels. For me, visits to these images, have become pilgrimages. Although much of the physical aspect of this life and this place are gone, I want to give it permanent real estate in my memory.

In 2014, on a trip to Atlantic City, I returned to the Claridge Hotel. This was before the devastating hurricane Sandy and the subsequent restoration. The hotel seemed frozen in time. Revisiting the deserted lobby, I found the old marble floors and columns, and the built out area where the newspapers, candy, cigars and small souvenirs were sold. I heard for the last time, in an atmosphere that seemed to be sleeping under a dome of glass, whispers of my lost youth, and of my romantic and beautiful privileged life.

I could suddenly picture the golden rolling carts and the gentlemen who would practically "hop" to do our bidding at the sound of a high bell. I could see the elegant desk and door attendants and, in the near distance, sense the pre-luncheon hustle of the semi-mysterious Meri Mayfair Lounge, and I could remember the opening and closing of the elevators, the rattling of the glass panes of the telephone booth doors, and the familiar sound of dress shoes crossing the polished floor.

In reality, this was me, roaming through the shadows of my life, joined in this passage by countless others in pursuit of reprise. Gathering under a dome, wearing glass slippers and dancing with phantom princes, fairy godmothers and Cinderellas. Together we waltzed in gorgeous skirts, formal uniforms and regalia—across the cool marble landscape, creating a new memory with every turn we executed, as we waited for the great hall clock to strike twelve.

The Million Dollar Pier

I am standing in a misty rain, on a cloud-covered ocean afternoon in front of the Million Dollar Pier. I may be awake or I may be dreaming. It doesn't matter.

Somehow, through the grey green mist what I hope for appears. The park has been closed down for years. Although what I experience in this afternoon in the melon air is memory, the brightness still comes through and I know that today the park has reawakened, especially for me. As in a dream, I am watching, knowing full well what comes next— I hold on to the gift this moment offers.

The images are vivid. I am standing there as if raindrops are falling down upon me. It is almost as if they are made of tiny pieces of paint from the colorful carousel horses. On these I travel in a circle to the sound of calliope music under the multitudinous bright bulbs and tilted mirrors. I am surrounded by all the celebrated rides: The Tea Cups, the red and yellow Tilt-a-Whirl, the Bumper Cars, the Ferris Wheel, and the Funhouse. I see all of the carnival games and stunts, the kewpie dolls, the stuffed animals and prizes. I can taste popcorn, candied apples, snow cones, cotton candy, and roasted peanuts.

I will always cherish thoughts of the afternoons and the evenings on the Million Dollar Pier with the clanging bells, the calliope, the sound of rides spinning, grinding, whirring, clattering and rising into the sky, but most of all, the laughter, and all of the people, so jubilant, so alive.

The Postcard Collection

I wonder how many of us sit in long sought out room-like apartments holding onto boxes of postcards from Atlantic City, New Jersey. How many fellow travelers are clutching cardboard boxes filled with a neon-bright world gone by?

The first in-color postcard made its debut in Atlantic City in 1893. Since that time there have been countless pictures taken, creating endless opportunities for collecting. It seems to me the old resort's high card is its history and provisioning of a haven for the employment and enjoyment for so many over time. It is difficult today to find a place in this city of troubled industry, as a transient, or as a permanent resident. It was easier in the old days, as I suppose many things were. Somehow the only true tenancy we can hope for now, in this environment of excitement, is accessed with fantasy. This occurs as we go through the windows, doorways and arches depicted in these small cards. In this way we take our places in the furniture we once occupied as kings and queens of the times these images bring to us . . . and remember.

To be fair, there is more to Atlantic City than what it once was. It is still a beautiful resilient strip along the sea. Waiting.

It could be a capital of preservation, of filmmaking, of individuals creating with the sense of artistry the place offers them with its water, air, weather, and history, capitalizing on a part of what it has been to millions of people since the middle of the 1800s. A place of creativity, glamour, business, transformation and mystery.

Perhaps there is a chance for it to turn around. Atlantic City's legacy could be more than what is left now in picture postcards of its past. A new bet is waiting like a promise, just as that barren swamp waited all of those years ago—to be counted in.

There is a Theatre

It is on a high floor of the old Chalfonte–Haddon Hall and it has been there since the late 1800s. On the top of the proscenium arch is a miniature three-masted clipper ship that always reminds me that we are all on a shared voyage. The theatre has seats and little attached side tables for dining. The interior decor is dark blue, burgundy, and gold and old-fashioned with ceilings that seem to soar to a sea foam marine heaven.

If I had my way, I would position myself on that rare, historic and unusual stage to pirouette in a shower of shimmering light in a grand red tulle evening gown, to tell my story. With the air of the sea just outside, I would breathe and stand in a misty column to offer a scarlet solo of thanksgiving to Atlantic City: "The Queen of Resorts." Perhaps in finding my story, I can bring part of it back. If I could live on a corner of this past, it would be on this one, on these boards, making a brief home in order to reclaim the pieces of myself that were lost long ago to the whispering tides and I would bear witness to the history of it all with my last aria.

It is hard to explain to those who have not seen it for themselves, what power the place held. Sometimes I can only sit and shake my head back and forth, nodding sideways, eyes shut, hoping I can hold onto what I remember and pray my heart will not break for the endless parade of images that come forth. I am an older person now, neither the hopeful child, nor the lovely young woman I became under the wing of this now elusive experience. I suppose there is only so much time one can spend on memory lane, before it becomes apparent it is time to move on to inhabit the present day.

I do know this, but feel as I take the walk to my last horizon, I want these old friends on my train: sea air, cotton candy, kewpie dolls, rolling carriages, Kodak family photos, ice cream vendors, salt water taffy and fudge, ocean beaches and seafood, glamour, dress up, souvenir shops, jewelry, suitcases, fountains of light, sand castles, violin serenades, movie stars and gangsters, Shirley Temples and venetian glassware, rhinestone earrings, dinner dresses, maître d's, hotel lobbies, salt water and fresh water tub bathing, amusement parks, rides to thrill like the Caterpillar and the Tilt-a-Whirl, tanning oil and Coppertone tans, diving horses, the entertainments and dancing at the Steel Pier, the Ice Capades and the Miss America Pageant, promenades on the boardwalk, snow cones, Mr. Peanut, walking on the beach, diamond rings, lavish dining and foods, movie going, tulle stoles and jeweled sweater sets, leather luggage pieces, hat boxes and train cases, hot dogs, frozen custard, conversations, and aerial advertisements . . . All an incomparable magical design for living.

There is a theatre high up in the old **Chalfonte–Haddon Hall**. There is a sailing ship thereabouts waiting to take me away. I know that as I walk toward it, down this earth, in my heavy gown, shedding one memory at a time, by the time I reach this home I, and it, will be light as feathers. I will have felt it, and said it, and worn it all. I will, unfettered by loss and grief, be free to set sail for my final, newly claimed, independent Hurrah!

After Words

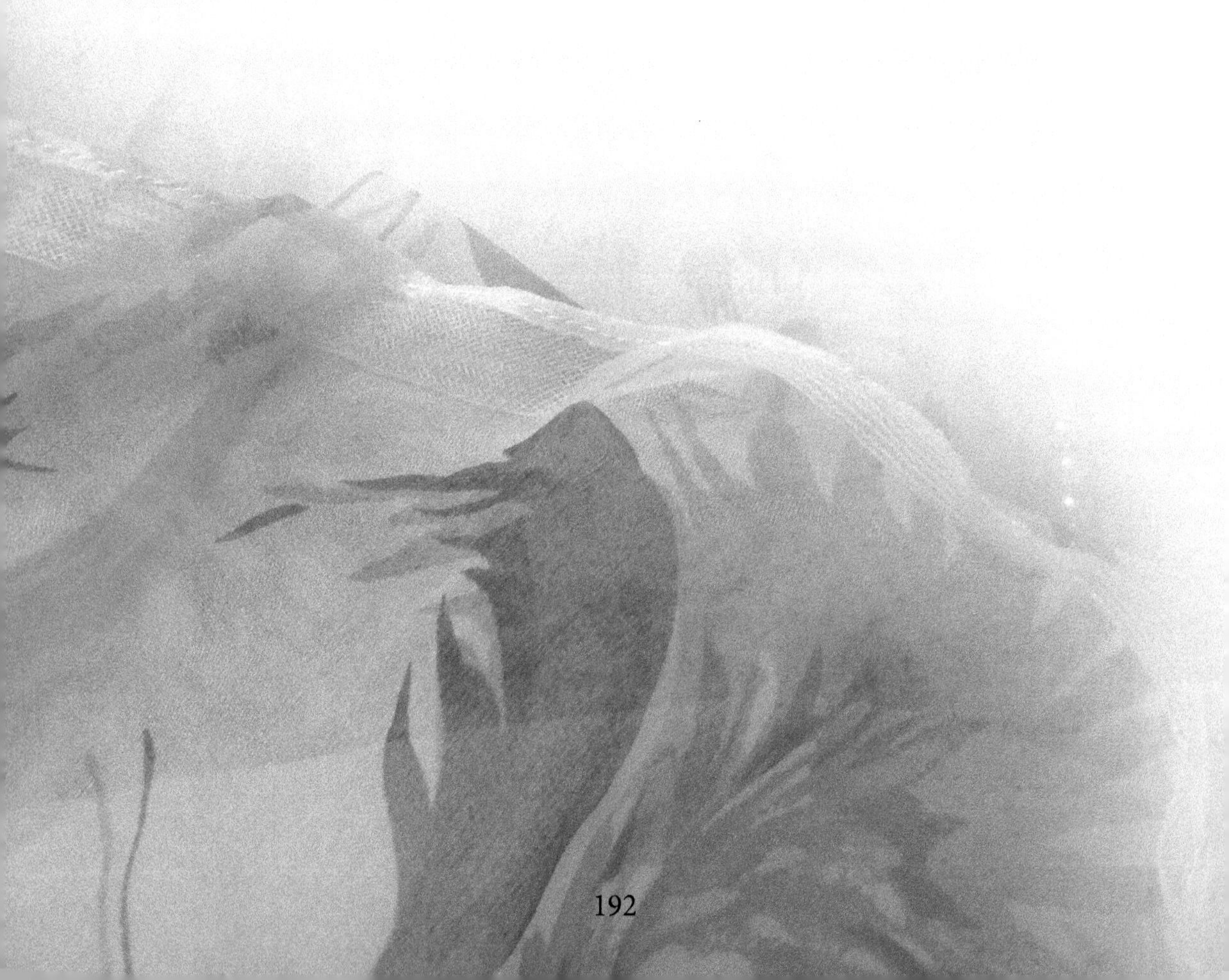

After Words

The Sea-Green Shower

The ending came way before we imagined it would. It was forecast, as, over the years, seasonal customs, and societal and political movements came and went. In my life, and in my summer experience with Atlantic City, the beginning was in the early 1950s and the slow collapse began in about 1963 when I was fifteen years old.

Cleopatra had been released and had failed. We had long ago been captivated by the riveting performances in John Huston's *Giant*. We had been entertained by lighthearted fare like *The Reluctant Debutante*, intrigued by William Inge's *Picnic,* exhilarated and shocked by *Elmer Gantry.* Then—all of a sudden—Alfred Hitchcock's film *Psycho* opened, and we were SCARED out of our wits. Now, here it was: the end. It was not the familiar ending of a vacation, season of study, friendship, or romance. This new loss was of innocence and of the hope that anything could remain the same. This was a cold shower raining on my youth. This was a startling, chilling, life-changing sea-green shimmer on the horizon. I probably spent the last season of my time in Atlantic City hiding under some roll-away bed in a dark green haze.

It is odd the movies ushered me out of the place I thought of as the theatre of my dreams, because it was the movies that had given me permission to dream in the first place.

When I look back on all of it, my triptych: losing my home in Spring Valley, losing the Tourist Home, and leaving Atlantic City, what I used to see was a deep chasm of sadness. Now, what I see is beauty. I still feel the familiar pain of loss, but it has been taken over by a new view of the dark and the light qualities that made it all so unique.

If someone were to ask, "What does it look like?" I would reply, almost hearing the strains of Purcell's aria from *Dido and Aeneas,* that, "When I am laid to rest," long after my final breath, I would look above and see a sight like the beautiful magnolia tree now above my head as it sheds its blooms one by one. I would see with gratitude and clarity, that for each falling bloom I carry a memory, and I would understand that each one has made me whole and ready to turn to the world with my song.

The Dinner Rings

I was at the Metropolitan Opera in New York City's Lincoln Center. The opera being performed that evening was *La Traviata* by Giuseppe Verdi. On this particular night, I was seated in a front row box in the Grand Tier on the left side of the house, and I happened to rest my hands on the railing. I was wearing a very dressy long black beaded gown. The shoes I wore were Charles Jourdan pumps, which I had long been saving for a special occasion.

As I looked down at my hands, I noticed the fourth finger of each one that, at one time, had worn diamond dinner rings. I remembered the first ring was in the shape of a rose window. It was delicate and had eight small diamonds surrounding the center. The rest of this ring was filled with tiny diamond chips. It was fashioned of intricately patterned white gold. The other ring was more traditional, rising from its white gold band to a square shape. The supports for this were lightly filigreed and held the central diamond with grace. I wore these rings from the time they were given to me, until I was 36 years old. It was then that I sold them to a pawn broker on Eighth Avenue, in New York City, around the corner from my Hell's Kitchen apartment. Until that moment, I had rarely taken them off. To me they were a symbol of adulthood and a legacy of loveliness from my Grandmother Letterman. By the time I had enough money to buy them back from the pawn shop, it had been torn down. My daily route, in those days, was to go downtown to my job on Wall Street at 26 Broadway, so I missed the store's uptown closing and I lost the rings.

As I looked down at my naked fingers on that winter night at the opera in the half light spilling from the orchestra pit, and heard the overture, so familiar to me by now, I mused, with a bowed head, how my own walk with music had begun.

I saw reflected, just inside of my eye, in a welling tear, the special moment when my Grandmother Letterman purchased these rings for me. The square ring was presented first. The rose window, purchased the same day, came into my possession later. But the moment of acquisition, etched permanently in my eyes, could not be washed away. I realized how much "going astray" in my own life had cost me. Love, marriage, a career, these rings, beauty. I was already, by then, on a path of personal recovery. Now, gazing at my folded hands, I knew the love could be saved, there might even be another wedding, or work to do, but the gorgeous diamond rings from the luxury boutique in the old colonnade of shops at Chalfonte–Haddon Hall, on the Atlantic City Boardwalk, would never, ever, return to me.

Somehow, as I listened to the music that evening, I felt my rings come alive again, delivered to me by the composition of this beautiful opera. As my eyes remained fixed upon the stage, I felt a sensation of warmth touching my fingers and realized that I did not need to own these pieces physically to experience them still. They were with me in the spirit of all of the lovely things that had become part of my life and, now, at the Metropolitan Opera, I discovered the real jewel in their memory.

The Opera Programs

A few years ago I participated in a regional flea market where I assembled old collectibles that reminded me of days gone by. One Sunday, a fellow vendor approached me with a stack of papers. He specialized in ephemera and said that this particular collection reminded him more of what might speak to me. I was touched by this consideration and accepted the gift of the packet of papers. I told him that I would enjoy looking at them later. As with many of my treasures, I put these items away for safe keeping and future review. I think this must have been a very busy time for me, for it was a year before I retrieved them from the drawer where I had put them. Then, in a private moment, I opened the bag I wrapped them in and looked attentively at what I drew from within.

What I now held in my hands were 36 programs from the touring company of The Metropolitan Opera. These were for the performances that took place at the Claridge Hotel in Atlantic City, New Jersey. The dates for the events spanned the years from 1946 until 1958. Even some of the names of the performers were familiar to me, as I had spent time in the world of opera.

These papers felt like a magic bundle in my hands and made me wonder how it came to be that I, with no particular background in music, had traveled such a path. It occurred to me that many of these experiences in life do come as gifts from seemingly magical quarters. It is also mysterious to realize that just where I stood or sat on a typical evening in our hotel's dining hall, many great opera stars of the day had performed.

I wondered if, somehow, I had received, from them, some inspiration or silent encouragement that would, in later years, enrich the experience I had as a stage director for opera, a dramatic coach, and even later still, for my few minutes as a singer. Outcomes and occurrences such as these remind me there is a dimension in life we do not see. It is powerful, persuasive, and often paves the way for important moments in private histories, thus shaping our personal operas.

Beyond Words

The Demolition of the Traymore

April 27, 1972

The ambient fires went out in my receiving rooms years ago. My shielding fireplace screens and fenders, still in place, are more fragile than they once were in their stalwart positions. Cold and worn, they are standing now, I believe, more out of a sense of duty and self respect. The carpets in my six hundred rooms are threadbare. The walls, as well, are shedding themselves of old paper and paint. Crystal sconces no longer glow in the darkness. The important furniture was taken from me long ago, but still, there are pieces in my guest rooms and in my lounges and dining rooms and marble entrance halls. These pieces, once carefully selected to complete my latent elegance, are now given little regard and have been abandoned to the ravages of time.

Hidden or tucked away in my distressed guest rooms are the last souvenirs of my visitors, the aristocracy of mid-19th to mid-20th century travel: a broken tiara on a lone boudoir table, a fading rose peignoir in a wardrobe trunk, old red dancing shoes, a painted lingerie chest filled with pale peach-colored silk, a multi-tiered mahogany button box spilling its bounty of miniature treasures, pairs of long white satin formal gloves, fraying French tulle evening gowns and bejeweled, if damaged, antique evening bags lying behind my curtains.

Perhaps there is even the ghostly figure of a man or a woman in one of my windows—waiting for romantic love to arrive or to depart. There are bent wire-rimmed spectacles and long ago emptied water glasses on the highboys. The air is musty and filled with the scent of old money.

My grand ballroom is redolent with the memory of thousands dancing and of their gaiety and theatrical splendor. In my hallways, eerie echoes of the immortal ocean breezes weave in and out of the glass transoms, still open, or even those that must have burst apart leaving showers of broken glass below their weathered frames like fallen tears.

I am looking now at my high golden-yellow rooftop domes—and waiting for the coming event.

It is April 27, 1972. I am ready.

I am reminiscing, looking down at the gardens in the block by the ocean. I am picturing my seaside patios with their lavish arrangements of flowers and fountains, with their greenery and walkways and pools, that created for my visitors an incomparable and gracious welcoming beauty.

As I brace myself for the coming moment, I am silenced by the enormity of my physical presence on this block and by the history of it all and ... now ... the unutterable ... devastation ...

The sadness that I feel for what might have been.

All my lights are out now.

It is time.

Raising my weary head to heaven and stretching my tired arms skyward, I let go. The explosion reaches my heart first. Thousands of my windows splinter and the broken panes fall like diamonds through the thick clouds of billowing pink smoke, producing wave after wave of shocking, smoldering, cascading rubble. My Dresden china, smashed to pieces, litters the mile-wide ground surface with newly fashioned place settings for signature breakfasts, luncheons, and lavish dinners and thus, now lies in wait for a new audience.

To this day I mourn the loss from my new home, deep below the surface, where I preside over unfalteringly loyal remains. Every evening, I rise from my long idyll to wander the perimeter of the now empty land in a glorious champagne-tulle high society gown with a crown of diamonds and pearls. Wrapped in illusion veiling, I pause and turn, only to look up in wonder at the empty air to recall the grandeur and occasion of my former role as the largest luxury hotel in the world: The Traymore.

Authors' Note

I am not sure when it happened, but somewhere along the line I became what I had lost. It was as if that which I had experienced in my life was defined only by the grief I felt and the heavy weight I carried. Somewhere along the line I became the houses, the hotels, and the people I had left behind.

The Traymore was such a place. Adjacent to the hotel where I stayed in Atlantic City for all the years of vacationing with my grandparents, it became a symbol of everything I treasured and wanted to become and when it was demolished—I went down with it.

Only now as I stand in the scarlet cinders of my past do I feel that I can shed these burdens, leaving the Traymore and all of the other losses behind in their graves by the sea. In so doing, I hope that I can take my own place in the days that remain to me, meeting them with a renewed lightness of heart and joy for what I've experienced, rather than sorrow for what no longer exists.

Your Words

About the Author

Martha Ann Letterman began directing in 1968. She has been recognized for her directorial skills in drama, musical theatre, opera and pieces from symphonic classical repertoire. Dramatic work included plays by Beckett, Pinter, Genet, Sartre and original scripts by playwrights Neal Bell and John O'Keefe. Opera directing included works by Offenbach, Stravinsky, Berio, Bizet, Puccini, Poulenc, Rachmaninoff, Mozart, Prokofiev, Argento, Tchaikovsky, Weill, Bellini, Gounod, Donizetti and Verdi.

The focal point of Martha's academic career was at the University of Iowa in Iowa City, Iowa. Here she received a Master of Fine Arts degree in Acting and Directing. Upon completion of her advanced degree, she was appointed as stage director for the Opera Theater and soon thereafter, additionally became Director of the Center for New Performing Arts. During this time she was privileged to work with distinguished faculty members from the dance, art, theatre, film, laser art technology, and music departments.

Highlights of her production work at Iowa were Prokofiev's *Love for Three Oranges*, a collaboration with stage designer Sam Kirkpatrick and San Diego-based director/writer and educator Paula Kalustian, *Paganini: Theresa's Dream*, an original theatre piece set to the music of Rachmaninoff's *Rhapsody on a Theme of Paganini* in collaboration with the Iowa Playwright's Workshop and stage designer Erik Ulfers, and an original dance theatre piece, *Lemon Cinders*, a collaboration with the Center for New Performing Arts and the University of Iowa Dance Department.

Martha directed on various professional and semi-professional stages across the United States, from The Huntington: Library, Art Collections, and Botanical Gardens in Pasadena, California, the Dorothy Chandler Pavilion in Los Angeles, to club performances in New York City, and The Barns at Wolf Trap in Vienna, Virginia. One of the special moments of her directing career was her concert staging of Poulenc's *La Voix Humaine* in collaboration with conductor James Conlon and soprano Jennifer Ringo at the Aspen Music Festival in Colorado.

She worked with artists from the Broadway Stage, the Metropolitan and City Operas, as well with as non-affiliated individuals. She served as a consultant to conductors, composers, managers, musicians, writers, coaches, singers and actors, assisting them with various aspects of their careers and personal paths.

Using her background as a performer she has found a direction that focuses on writing and speaking. She creates and presents Private Theatre in various intimate venues, using poetry, anecdotes, and observations she has gathered along her journey of life.

Scarlet Cinders, Martha's first book, developed as a series of vignettes for performance, is a response to her need to create a personal milestone. Continuing from here, she is working on a collection entitled: *Where is Bluefield? The Real Estate,* where she tells stories relating to her adventures looking for places to live and looking at houses in towns across the United States of America.

Martha now lives in Cumberland, Maryland. She enjoys the opportunity to travel to Washington, DC, her hometown, and to New York City where she continues her work as a consultant.